WriteTraits®

TEACHER'S GUIDE

Vicki Spandel

Grade 6

GReaT S⚫uRCe®
EDUCATION GROUP
A Houghton Mifflin Company

Vicki Spandel

Vicki Spandel was codirector of the original teacher team that developed the six-trait model and has designed instructional materials for all grade levels. She has written several books, including *Creating Writers—Linking Writing Assessment and Instruction* (Longman), and is a former language arts teacher, journalist, technical writer, consultant, and scoring director for dozens of state, county, and district writing assessments.

Cover: Illustration by Claude Martinot Design.

Printed in the United States of America

International Standard Book Number: 0-669-49045-8

1 2 3 4 5 6 7 8 9 10 - MZ - 07 06 05 04 03 02

Contents

Introduction

Unit 1: Ideas

Unit 2: Organization

Unit 3: Voice

Unit 4: Word Choice

Unit 5: Sentence Fluency

Unit 6: Conventions

Welcome to the World of Traits!

With the Write Traits® Classroom Kit, we offer you a way of teaching writing that helps students understand what good writing is and how to achieve it. The kit provides instruction in six traits of effective writing. The term *trait*, as it is used here, refers to a characteristic or quality that defines writing. The six traits of writing, as defined by teachers themselves, are these:

- Ideas
- Organization
- Voice
- Word Choice
- Sentence Fluency
- Conventions

Six-trait writing is based on the premise that students who become strong self-assessors become better writers and revisers, and we are quite certain that you will find this to be true. No matter where your student writers are right now, we are sure you will see improvements in their skills. You will also see them gain the confidence that comes from knowing writer's language and having options for revision.

Components in the Write Traits® Classroom Kit

Each *Write Traits® Classroom Kit* contains the following components:

Teacher's Guide

The Teacher's Guide takes you step-by-step through each part of the program, from introducing the traits to presenting lessons to wrap-up activities that bring all traits together. Also contained in the Teacher's Guide are 6-point and 5-point reproducible rubrics and sample papers to practice scoring.

Student Traitbook

Available as a copymaster within the kit or for purchase for every student, the Student Traitbook contains all the practice exercises for the six traits.

Posters

Hang the two posters for students to use as a handy reference when revising their writing.

Self-stick Note Pads (package of 5)

Use these handy self-stick notes to indicate your scoring and comments so that you won't have to write directly on students' papers.

Overhead Transparencies

Use the transparencies for whole-class scoring or for discussion of the sample papers found in the back of the Teacher's Guide.

Writing Pockets

Available for purchase for every student, these writing packets serve as a reminder to students of the six traits and as a place to store their writing in progress.

Teaching the Traits units

The Teacher's Guide is organized into six units, one for each of the six traits. Each unit includes an overview, four lessons specifically designed to build strengths in that trait, and a unit wrap-up. At the end of the book are sample papers to use for practice in scoring papers.

Unit Overviews

Each of the six unit overviews accomplishes the following:

- defines the trait

- lists the instruction that will be emphasized

- provides a summary of each lesson

- contains two 6-point rubrics for scoring papers on the trait (one for the teacher, one for the student)

- recommends literature that can be used to model the trait

Traits Lessons

All twenty-four lessons, four for each of the six traits, follow the same format:

- Introduction, which includes an objective, skills focus, and suggested time frame

- Setting Up the Lesson, which introduces the main concepts of the lesson

- Teaching the Lesson, which provides teaching suggestions and answers for material in the Student Traitbook

- Extending the Lesson, which offers optional activities that carry the lesson concepts beyond the *Write Traits®* *Classroom Kit*

Unit Summaries

Each of the six unit summaries does the following:

• reviews the characteristics of the trait

• looks at the rubric

• applies the rubric to scoring sample papers

Warm-up and Wrap-up Activities

Warm-up activities are provided to help you introduce the concept of traits *("What is a trait?")* and the concept of analyzing writing by allowing students to assess right from the start. Warm-up activities help students think like writers and heighten their awareness of the traits within writing samples. The wrap-up activities are designed to show you whether students have a full grasp of the traits and can use all six of them together.

Using Rubrics To Score Papers

Rubrics and Checklists

Please note that a checklist is NOT a rubric. The checklist included on your kit poster simply offers students a convenient way of reviewing their writing to make sure that they have not forgotten any important elements of revision. The checklist includes no numbers and does not define performance at various levels along a rating scale. For this reason, neither you nor the students should use the checklist to assign scores.

Differences Between Rubrics

Our kit includes two 6-point rubrics for each trait, one for you and one for your students. We recognize that across the country, 4-, 5-, and 6-point scales are all in use. All have advantages. We believe, however, that the 6-point rubric reflects the greatest range of performance while still requiring raters to choose between generally strong papers (4s, 5s, or 6s) and papers in need of serious revision (1s, 2s, or 3s).

The 6-point rubric allows the assigning of an "above expectations" score of 6. Further, it divides the midpoint portion of the scoring range into two scores: 3 and 4. Think of a score of 3 on a 6-point rubric as a midrange performance, but one with a few more *weaknesses* than *strengths.* A score of 4, on the other hand, while also a midrange performance, has a few more *strengths* than *weaknesses.*

However, for your convenience we have also included 5-point rubrics, both teacher and student versions, in the appendix at the back of this Teacher's Guide.

Scoring Sample Papers

Sample papers included in this kit have been carefully selected to match precisely or very closely the grade level at which your students are writing. Some papers are informational; others are narrative. Some are well done; others reflect moderate to serious need for revision. These "in process" papers offer an excellent opportunity for students to practice revision skills on the work of others, and we recommend that you ask students to practice revising as many papers as time permits. This extended practice provides an excellent lead-in to the revision of their own work.

Suggested scores based on a 6-point rubric are provided for each paper. (Scores based on the 5-point rubric are in the appendix.) These scores are just that—*suggestions.* They reflect the thoughtful reading and assessment of trained teachers, but they should not be considered correct "answers." While no score is final, any score must be defensible, meaning that the scorer can defend it using the language of the rubric.

Frequently Asked Questions

How did this six-trait approach get started?

The *Write Traits® Classroom Kit* is based upon the six-trait model of writing instruction and assessment that teachers in the Beaverton, Oregon, School District developed in 1984. Because it has been so widely embraced by teachers at all grade levels, kindergarten through college, the model has since spread throughout the country—and much of the world. Traits themselves, of course, have been around as long as writing; writers have always needed intriguing ideas, good organization, a powerful voice, and so on. What is *new* is using consistent language with students to define writing at various levels of performance.

As a teacher, how can I make this program work for my students?

You can do several important things:

- Look to your students for answers; let them come up with their own ideas about what makes writing work, rather than simply giving them answers.

- Encourage students to be assessors and to verbalize their responses to many pieces of writing, including other students' work, professional writing, and your writing.

- Be a writer yourself, modeling steps within the writing process and encouraging students to use their increasing knowledge of the traits to coach you.

- Give students their own writing rubrics as you introduce each trait. Use the rubrics to assess writing and to help students see those rubrics as guides to revision.

- Share copies of rubrics with parents, too. This sharing encourages their involvement and helps them understand precisely how their children's writing is assessed.

Does six-trait instruction/assessment take the place of the writing process?

Absolutely not! The six-trait approach is meant to enhance and enrich a process-based approach to writing. Along with a wide set of options for revising, it gives students a language for talking and thinking like writers. Often students do not revise their writing thoroughly (or at all) because they have no idea what to do. Students who know the six traits have no difficulty thinking of ways to revise writing.

What do I do if I don't know a lot about the writing process?

Don't worry. We can help. First, you may wish to read the brief article by Jeff Hicks that summarizes the writing process. It appears on page xv of this Teacher's Guide and will give you all the basic information and terminology you need to work your way through the lessons without difficulty. If you would like to know more, refer to the Teacher Resources, page xviii. These resources will give you a strong background in the basics of the writing process, even if you've never been to a single workshop on the subject!

What do I have to give up from my current curriculum?

Nothing. If you are teaching writing through writers' workshops or any writing process–based approach, you will find that virtually everything you do is completely compatible with this program. It is ideally suited to process writing and particularly supports the steps of revision and editing.

Do I have to teach the traits in order?

We recommend that you teach both traits and lessons in the order presented because we use a sequential approach in which skills build on one another. Longer writing activities toward the end of each trait unit will require students to use the skills they have learned in studying a previous trait so that nothing is "lost." In other words, we do not want students to forget about *ideas* just because they move on to *organization.*

We do recognize, though, that most teachers prefer to teach conventions throughout the course of instruction, rather than as a separate unit. Therefore, incorporate instruction in conventions as you present the other traits.

Do all six traits ever come together?

Definitely. Writing should not be disjointed. We take it apart (into traits) to help students *master specific strategies for revision.* But eventually, we must put the slices of the pie back together. With this in mind, we provide several closure lessons, including one in which students will score a paper for all six traits and check their results with those of a partner. By this time, students will also be ready to assess and revise their own writing for all six traits. Wrap-up lessons may be assessed if you choose to do so.

Using Traits with the Writing Process

by Jeff Hicks

If writing were an act of fairy-tale magic or a matter of wishing, the word *process* would never apply to what people do when they write. All writers would have to do is wave their magic wands, rub their enchanted lamps to make their genies appear, or catch the one fish—from an ocean filled with fish—that grants wishes to the lucky person who hauls it in. *I'd like a bestseller about a pig and a spider who live on a farm. Allakazam! Presto! Newbery Medal!* Perhaps Roald Dahl was a fisherman and Beverly Cleary was a collector of antique lamps, right? Of course not! Writers understand that writing is a process involving multiple steps and plenty of time. An understanding of the process of writing is an important foundation for all young writers. Once they have the process in place, students can grasp and use the six traits of writing to help them revise and assess their own work. The six traits support the writing process.

The Writing Process The traditional view of the writing process is one that involves four or five steps or stages.

> **Prewriting**
> **Drafting (Writing)**
> **Revising**
> **Editing**
> **Publishing/Sharing**

1. **Prewriting**—This is the stage in which the writer attempts to find a topic, narrow it, and map out a plan. The writer usually isn't concerned with creating whole sentences or paragraphs at this point. Prewriting is done *before* the writer begins to write, and it is aimed at defining an idea and getting it rolling.

2. **Drafting** (Writing)—In this stage, the writer's idea begins to come to life. Sentences and paragraphs begin to take shape. The writer may experiment with different leads. In this stage, writers need to know that they can change directions, cross out words or sentences, and draw arrows to link details that are out of sequence. The term *rough draft*, or *first draft*, refers to writers in motion, changing directions and letting their ideas take shape.

3. **Revising**—When writers revise, their topics and ideas come into focus. In this stage, writers do a great deal of math—adding or subtracting single words, phrases, or entire paragraphs. What to revise often becomes clearer to students if they have had some time away from their drafts. Putting a draft away, out of sight and mind, for a few days or even more, may provide a sharper focus on weak areas. A writer might even ask, "Did I really write this?" The efforts made at revision will easily separate strong writing from weak writing.

4. **Editing**—This stage is all about making a piece of writing more accessible to readers. In this stage, writers fine-tune their work by focusing on correct punctuation, capitalization, grammar, usage, and paragraphing. Writers will want to be open to all the technological help (spell checking, for example) and human help they can find.

5. **Publishing/Sharing**—Not every piece of writing reaches this stage. The term *sharing* refers here to something more public than the kind of interactive sharing that should be happening at the previous stages. When writing is going to be "published" in the classroom or put on display as finished work, it needs to have been carefully selected as a piece of writing that has truly experienced all the other stages of the writing process.

These steps are often presented in classrooms as being separate, mutually exclusive events. *If I'm prewriting, I can't be revising. If I'm drafting, I can't be editing. If I'm revising, I can't be editing.* Mature writers know that the process may proceed through the steps in linear fashion, one at a time, but it is more likely that the parts of the process will intertwine. The process doesn't seem so overwhelming if a young writer can gain this perspective. I like to teach students several prewriting strategies—webbing, outlining, making word caches, drawing, and developing a list of questions—but I also like to show them through my own writing that prewriting and drafting can occur simultaneously. Having students experience their teacher as a writer is the most powerful way to demonstrate the importance of each stage and how it connects with the others. For instance, the best way for me to prewrite is to begin "writing." It is the act of writing (drafting) that often gets my ideas flowing better than if I tried to make a web of the idea. Writing also allows me to demonstrate that I can revise at any time. I can cross out a sentence, change a word, draw an arrow to place a sentence in a different paragraph, add a few words, or move a whole paragraph; all of this can be done while I draft an idea. At the same time, I might even notice that I need to fix the spelling of a word or add a period—that's editing!

Bringing in the Traits I know that many young writers speak and act as if they have magical pens or pencils. In the classroom, these are the students who proclaim, "I'm done!" minutes after beginning, or they are the ones who say, "But I like it the way it is!" when faced with a teacher's suggestion to tell a bit more or to make a few changes. Other students frequently complain, "I don't have anything to write about." Immersing these students in the writing process with a teacher who is also a writer is the clearest path to silencing these comments. Throw into this mix a strong understanding of the six traits of writing, and you are well on your way to creating passionate, self-assessing writers.

Teacher Resources

The "Must-Have" List for Teaching Writing
Using the Six Traits

Ballenger, Bruce. 2000. *The Curious Researcher: A Guide to Writing Research Papers.* Needham Heights, MA: Allyn & Bacon.

Blake, Gary and Robert W. Bly. 1993. *The Elements of Technical Writing.* New York: Macmillan.

Calkins, Lucy McCormick. 1994. *The Art of Teaching Writing,* 2nd ed. Portsmouth, NH: Heinemann.

Claggett, Fran, et al. 1999. *Daybook of Critical Reading and Writing* (Grade 6). Wilmington, MA: Great Source Education Group, Inc.

Fletcher, Ralph and Joann Portalupi. 1998. *Craft Lessons: Teaching Writing K through 8.* Portland, Maine: Stenhouse Publishers.

Fox, Mem. 1993. *Radical Reflections: Passionate Opinions on Teaching, Learning, and Living.* New York: Harcourt Brace & Company.

Frank, Marjorie. 1995. *If You're Trying to Teach Kids How to Write . . .: You've Gotta Have This Book!* 2nd ed. Nashville: Incentive Publications, Inc.

Glynn, Carol. 2001. *Learning on Their Feet: A Sourcebook for Kinesthetic Learning Across the Curriculum K–8.* Shoreham, VT: Discover Writing Press.

Harvey, Stephanie. 1998. *Nonfiction Matters: Reading, Writing, and Research in Grades 3–8.* Portland, ME: Stenhouse Publishers.

Lamott, Anne. 1995. *Bird by Bird: Some Instructions on Writing and Life.* New York: Alfred A. Knopf.

Lane, Barry. 1998. *The Reviser's Toolbox.* Shoreham, VT: Discover Writing Press.

Murray, Donald M. 1990. *A Writer Teaches Writing.* 2nd ed. New York: Houghton Mifflin.

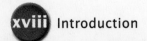

O'Conner, Patricia T. 1999. *Words Fail Me: What Everyone Who Writes Should Know About Writing.* New York: Harcourt Brace & Company.

Portalupi, Joann, with Ralph Fletcher. 2001. *Nonfiction Craft Lessons Teaching Information Writing K–8.* Portland, Maine: Stenhouse Publishers.

Sebranek, Patrick, et al. 1999. *Write Source 2000: A Guide to Writing, Thinking, and Learning.* Wilmington, MA: Great Source Education Group, Inc.

Spandel, Vicki. 2001. *Creating Writers,* 3rd ed. New York: Allyn & Bacon.

Stiggins, Richard J. 1996. *Student-Centered Classroom Assessment,* 2nd ed. Columbus, OH: Prentice Hall (Merrill).

Thomason, Tommy. 1998. *Writer to Writer: How to Conference Young Authors.* Norwood, MA: Christopher-Gordon Publishers.

Thomason, Tommy and Carol York. 2000. *Write on Target: Preparing Young Writers to Succeed on State Writing Achievement Tests.* Norwood, MA: Christopher Gordon Publishers.

Using Write Traits Classroom Kits
with *Write Source 2000*

Write Traits Classroom Kit, Grade 6	Skill Focus	*Write Source 2000* © 1999
Unit 1: Ideas		
Lesson 1: Draw on the Count of Three	Use prewriting strategies	Prewriting: Choosing a Subject, pp. 45–60
Lesson 2: Narrowing Your Topic	Narrow the topic	Planning Your Writing, p. 59
Lesson 3: From Fuzzy to Focused	Focus the writing	Prewriting: Choosing a Subject, p. 10
Lesson 4: That's Pretty Sketchy!	Include enough details	Prewriting: Gathering Details, p. 11
Unit 2: Organization		
Lesson 5: Name That Pattern!	Identify organizational patterns	Methods of Organization, p. 60
Lesson 6: The Right Tool for the Job	Match the pattern to the task	Revising for Organization, p. 71
Lesson 7: Building Bridges: Connecting Ideas	Use transitions	Transitions, p. 106
Lesson 8: Putting It All Together	Organize a paragraph	The Parts of a Paragraph, pp. 98–99
Unit 3: Voice		
Lesson 9: Defining Voice	Define voice	Engaging Voice, p. 22
Lesson 10: Voice in Expository Writing	Match voice to the task	Writing Guidelines (Expository Essays), pp. 110–111
Lesson 11: "Hello, How Are You?" or "Waz Up?"	Match voice to the audience	Five Keys to Good Revision, p. 69

Lesson 12: From Flat to Fantastic	Revise to enhance voice	Revising for Voice, pp. 72–73
Unit 4: Word Choice		
Lesson 13: Feeding Your Reader's Brain	Use sensory language	Using Strong Colorful Words, p. 135
Lesson 14: Word Graphics	Expand word knowledge	Improving Your Vocabulary, pp. 323–340
Lesson 15: Specify to Clarify	Use specific language	Developing a Sense of Style, p. 130
Lesson 16: Cut the Clutter!	Cut out unnecessary words	Checking for Word Choice, p. 82
Unit 5: Sentence Fluency		
Lesson 17: Short, Long, and In-between	Vary sentence length	Combining Sentences, p. 74
Lesson 18: Catching Up with Run-on Sentences	Eliminate run-on sentences	Composing Sentences, pp. 85–92
Lesson 19: From First to Last in Fluency	Revise text for fluency	Checking for Sentence Smoothness, p. 81
Lesson 20: What Makes It Flow?	Examine elements that contribute to fluency	Smooth-Reading Sentences, p. 23
Unit 6: Conventions		
Lesson 21: Revising, Editing, or "Revisediting"?	Differentiate revising and editing	One Writer's Process, pp. 9–18
Lesson 22: The Editor's Code	Use editor's marks	Editing and Proofreading Marks, inside back cover
Lesson 23: Eyes, Ears, Rules, and Tools	Identify errors	Editing and Proofreading, pp. 79–82
Lesson 24: A Personalized Checklist	Make an editing checklist	Editing and Proofreading Checklist, p. 83

Write Traits® Classroom Kits
SCOPE AND SEQUENCE

Trait/Skill	Grade					
	3	4	5	6	7	8
IDEAS						
Narrowing the Topic			•	•	•	•
Getting Started	•	•		•		•
Identifying the Main Idea	•	•	•			
Clarifying Ideas				•	•	•
Expanding Sketchy Writing			•	•	•	
Identifying What Is Important	•	•	•			
Making Writing Concise	•	•			•	•
ORGANIZATION						
Writing a Strong Lead	•	•	•			
Putting Things in Order	•		•		•	
Identifying Organizational Patterns		•		•		•
Matching Organizational Pattern and Writing Task		•		•		•
Staying on Topic	•		•		•	
Creating Strong Transitions				•	•	•
Writing Endings	•	•	•			
Putting Details Together				•	•	•
VOICE						
Defining Voice				•	•	•
Matching Voice and Purpose	•		•		•	
Putting Voice into Personal Narrative	•	•	•			
Putting Voice into Expository Writing				•	•	•
Matching Voice to Audience				•	•	•
Sharing Favorite Voices	•	•	•			
Putting Voice into Flat Writing		•		•		•
Using Personal Voice	•	•	•			

Trait/Skill	Grade					
	3	4	5	6	7	8
WORD CHOICE						
Using Strong Verbs	•	•	•			
Using Synonyms and Antonyms to Enhance Meaning				•	•	•
Inferring Meaning from Context	•	•	•			
Using Sensory Words to Create a Word Picture	•	•	•	•		•
Using Strong Words to Revise Flat Writing				•	•	•
Revising Overwritten Language		•		•	•	•
Eliminating Wordiness	•		•		•	
SENTENCE FLUENCY						
Making Choppy Writing Fluent	•		•		•	
Varying Sentence Beginnings	•	•				•
Varying Sentence Length			•	•	•	
Eliminating Run-ons	•	•		•		
Inserting Transitions				•	•	•
Creating Dialogue	•	•	•			
Assessing Fluency Through Interpretive Reading		•		•		•
Reading and Revising Personal Text			•		•	•
CONVENTIONS						
Distinguishing Between Revising and Editing		•	•	•	•	•
Spotting Errors	•		•		•	
Knowing the Symbols	•	•	•	•	•	•
Correcting Errors	•	•	•	•	•	•
Creating an Editing Checklist	•	•		•		•

Before beginning these activities, make sure students understand that a trait helps define any concept, such as writing or cooking. Activity 1 involves students in the act of assessing writing. As you discuss the ranking of the writing pieces with students, emphasize the language of the traits. Activity 2 is an activity for students who are not familiar with the definitions of the six traits of writing. Warm-up Activity 1 will take about 35 minutes. Warm-up Activity 2 should take about 10 minutes and does not have accompanying Student Traitbook pages.

Warm-up Activity 1

Ranking Three Papers

For use with Student Traitbook pages 5–6.

This is an extended warm-up activity, designed to sharpen students' skills as assessors and help them identify specifically what makes a piece of writing strong or weak. Students will not score these samples but will rank them from strongest to weakest and discuss their differences. In students' discussions, you will very likely hear the language of the traits even if you have not introduced them yet.

Students will read three versions of the writer's informational piece on polar bears. As you will see, the pieces differ in quality and extent of detail, completeness of organizational structure, word choice, and voice. Conventions are quite strong in all examples because the purpose of the activity is to get students to think beyond conventions to the other elements that make writing work.

Tell students to make marks on the samples as you read aloud or as they read silently. Suggest that they circle or underline parts that stand out because they are weak or strong. After reading or listening to each paragraph, students should use their marks to help them decide which paragraph is the strongest and which is the weakest. They should give reasons for ranking the papers in a particular way.

Ask students to share their rankings (record these on an overhead) and to briefly explain their reasons.

Rationales for Ranking

Students should see Sample 3 as the strongest. It has an excellent lead and conclusion and is well-organized. It has a main theme and supports this theme with rich details. The writer seems enthusiastic about the topic, which gives great voice to this informational piece. Notice also the strong word choice, including *swirling, formidable, soaking up heat, superb hunter,* and *potential prey.* Sentence beginnings and lengths are also widely varied.

Students should see Sample 1 as the next strongest. Though it lacks the detail of Sample 3, it does provide a fairly clear picture of life for the polar bear. Sample 1 has many "details," but they are more general than those provided in Sample 3. Still, it is clearly presented. The organizational structure of this piece is somewhat random; there is no strong central theme, as in Sample 3. Facts are tossed at readers, and there is redundancy, especially of the notion that polar bears are dangerous. The lead and conclusion are present, each emphasizing that the polar bear is "interesting" but not explaining how. The writer seems partially engaged, so voice is present but not powerful. A few examples of good word choice stand out: *highly valued, terrorizing a village.* Fluency is kept at a modest level because too many sentences begin with "Polar bears" or "The polar bear."

Sample 2 is certainly the most in need of revision. It is extremely general and has no real theme or sense of direction. It has a lead but no real conclusion. Because of its fact-upon-fact approach, the voice is minimal. Word choice is adequate but not exciting. Sentence beginnings are somewhat varied, but the lengths are very similar, adding to the monotony. The tone and approach are quite mundane, and the writer has not provided any bits of information that could make this expository piece intriguing to a reader. In some cases, the writer seems to be searching for information merely to fill space or time—not to educate the audience.

Defining the Traits of Good Writing

For beginning students, this activity is an opportunity to learn the six traits. For students with previous trait-based instruction, this warm-up serves as an excellent review. Display a list of the traits on the board or on an overhead transparency. Have students number a sheet of paper from 1 through 6. Tell students to listen as you read aloud each definition and then to write the name of the trait that matches the definition.

1. This trait is of particular interest to writers who are concerned that errors in spelling, capitalization, and grammar could get in the way of meaning. *(conventions)*

2. This trait shows the writer's confidence, enthusiasm for the topic, and sensitivity to the audience. *(voice)*

3. This trait is about making a topic small enough to handle yet including enough details to let the reader picture what the writer is talking about. *(ideas)*

4. This trait encourages the use of strong verbs and sensory words that help the reader see, hear, smell, taste, and feel the writer's experience. *(word choice)*

5. This is a trait you sense with your ears as much as with your eyes. It helps writing flow smoothly. *(sentence fluency)*

6. This trait depends on masterful beginnings and endings but also concerns the overall structure or pattern evident in a piece of writing. *(organization)*

WriteTraits®
TEACHER'S GUIDE

Overview

This unit introduces the concept of ideas—understanding what contributes good, strong ideas in a piece of writing and working with ideas to shape and improve them. Students will practice two strategies for prewriting (drawing and using detail "bricks"), narrow a sprawling topic, identify problems with fuzzy writing, and transform sketchy, dull writing into a piece capable of holding a reader's attention.

The focus of the instruction in this unit will be
- helping students develop new prewriting strategies
- giving students practice in narrowing a big topic to manageable size
- showing students how to transform fuzzy writing into focused writing
- helping students create writing that will keep readers "tuned in"

Ideas: A Definition

Ideas are all about information. In a strong creative piece, ideas paint a picture in the reader's mind. In an informational piece, strong ideas make difficult or complex information easy to understand. Three things make ideas work well, and they should be the focus of your instruction: *a main idea* that's easy to identify and narrow enough to be manageable, *interesting details* that bring the main idea to life, and *clarity*, which is achieved in part through the careful selection and presentation of important details. Finally, good writing always includes details about those beyond-the-obvious bits of information that thoughtful, observant writers notice.

The Unit at a Glance

The following lessons in the Teacher's Guide and practice exercises in the Student Traitbook will help develop understanding of the trait of ideas. The Unit Summary provides an opportunity to practice evaluating papers for the trait of ideas.

Unit Overview: Ideas

Teacher's Guide pages 2–6   The unique features of the trait of ideas are presented along with a rubric and a list of recommended literature for teaching ideas.

Lesson 1: Draw on the Count of Three

Teacher's Guide pages 7–9
Student Traitbook pages 8–11   In this lesson, students learn to use two prewriting strategies: first, they create a simple sketch to help generate and clarify details; second, they use detail "bricks" to begin building a solid picture in the reader's mind.

Lesson 2: Following the Signs to a Manageable Topic

Teacher's Guide pages 10–12
Student Traitbook pages 12–15   The purpose of the lesson is to provide practice in narrowing a huge topic to a manageable size.

Lesson 3: From Fuzzy to Focused

Teacher's Guide pages 13–15
Student Traitbook pages 16–19   This lesson is designed to help students identify the specific kinds of language writers use to make writing precise and then to emulate that technique by turning fuzzy samples into focused writing.

Lesson 4: That's Pretty Sketchy!

Teacher's Guide pages 16–18
Student Traitbook pages 20–23   This lesson helps students find specific strategies to create writing that keeps readers "tuned in."

Unit Summary: Ideas

Teacher's Guide page 19
Overhead numbers 1–4   Use the student rubric on page 5 and the activities in the Summary to practice evaluating writing for the trait of ideas. Remember, 5-point rubrics, along with rationales for scores on sample papers, appear in the Appendix of this Teacher's Guide on pages 192–214.

Teacher Rubric for Ideas

6
- The paper is clear and focused from beginning to end. The topic is small and very well defined, so it's easy for the writer to manage.
- The message/story is both engaging and memorable.
- The writer seems to have in-depth understanding of the topic.
- The writer is selective, consistently sharing unusual, beyond-the-obvious details that are informative, entertaining, or both.

5
- This paper makes sense throughout. It is clear—never confusing. The topic is small enough to handle in the scope of the paper.
- The message/story has many engaging moments.
- The writer knows enough about the topic to do a thorough job.
- The writer has chosen many interesting or little-known details.

4
- The reader can tell what the writer's main idea is. The topic is fairly well defined, but it needs to be narrower and more manageable.
- The message/story has some engaging moments.
- The writer knows the topic reasonably well; more information would make this writing more interesting and/or helpful.
- The writing includes some interesting or unusual details.

3
- It is fairly easy to *guess* what the main idea is. Some parts are unclear, however, or the topic is still too big to handle.
- The message/story lacks engaging moments.
- Sometimes the writer appears to know what he or she is talking about; at other times, the writer seems to struggle just to fill the page.
- Detail is present, but some details are very general.

2
- The main idea is unclear. What is this writer trying to say?
- The message/story has no engaging moments.
- The writer seems to be writing mainly to fill space.
- Details are very sketchy. The reader can only guess at the writer's meaning.

1
- This writer is still searching for a main idea—or story. It's not there yet.
- The writing is too sketchy to have a main idea, or it consists of random thoughts or notes that share no apparent common theme.
- The message/story has no engaging moments.
- The reader cannot extract anything meaningful, even by guessing.

Student Rubric for Ideas

6
- My paper is crystal clear from the first sentence to the last. It is very easy to tell what my main idea is.
- Every detail relates plainly to my main idea. My paper is focused.
- I know this topic well, and the reader can tell that by reading my paper.
- I was careful to choose interesting, unusual details that would keep readers reading.

5
- This paper makes sense. It is not confusing or vague. I think this topic is well-defined and manageable; it's not too big.
- Almost everything I write relates to my main idea.
- I know quite a bit about this topic.
- Most of my details go beyond the obvious. The reader may gain some insight or learn one or two interesting things by reading.

4
- The reader can tell what my main idea is. I may have a moment of confusing or vague writing. This topic still needs to be smaller.
- Most of what I write relates to my main idea.
- I know some things about this topic. If I knew more, or if I'd thought about it more, the paper would be stronger.
- Some interesting or unusual details stand out. At other moments, I let my writing get too general, or I repeated things.

3
- The reader can probably guess what my main idea is. Some parts are not clear, though. I think it would help to make this topic smaller.
- Some of this information isn't really related to my main idea.
- I needed to know more about this topic to do a really good job.
- I have a few interesting details, but the reader must hunt for them. A lot of this writing is general information everyone knows.

2
- My main idea is hard to figure out. I think the reader will wonder what it is I am trying to say. Maybe my topic is too big—or it's just unclear.
- A lot of this information does not relate to my main idea.
- I do not know much about my topic. Mostly I wrote to fill space.
- I need a lot more detail. This does not say much.

1
- I do not even *have* a main idea. I wrote whatever came into my head.
- This is just a list of facts or events.
- This is unclear and confusing. Most readers will not keep reading.
- I really don't include any details.

Recommended Literature for Teaching Ideas

Ask students questions like these when you read all or part of a book: *What do you picture in your mind as you listen? Do these characters seem like real people? Is this information clear? What strategies did the author use to make this writing work?*

Claggett, Fran, Louann Reid, and Ruth Vinz. 1999. *Daybook of Critical Reading and Writing, Grade 6.* Wilmington, MA: Great Source Education Group, Inc. Outstanding excerpts from the best of modern literature combine with challenging writing tasks that touch on numerous ideas-related skills.

Facklam, Margery. 2001. *Spiders and Their Web sites.* Boston: Little, Brown & Company. Excellent use of unusual detail, well presented.

Jackson, Donna M. 2000.*The Wildlife Detectives: How Forensic Scientists Fight Crimes Against Nature (Scientists in the Field).* Boston: Houghton Mifflin. Well-researched information that's fresh and makes good use of important details.

Locker, Thomas. 1998. *Home: A Journey Through America.* New York: Harcourt. Striking details create powerful images and feelings in these poems and bits of prose from many of America's most cherished writers.

Morgenstern, Susie. 1998. *Secret Letters From 0 to 10.* Translation copy (from French) New York: Penguin Putnam Inc. Exceptional use of showing, not telling, to achieve character development.

Sebranek, Patrick, Dave Kemper and Verne Meyer. 1999. *Write Source 2000.* Wilmington, MA: Great Source Education Group, Inc. Information on gathering ideas, identifying a main idea, using graphic organizers, making use of sensory details, and much more related to the trait of ideas.

Wallace, Barbara Brooks. 1985. *Peppermints in the Parlor.* New York: Simon & Schuster. Creative combinations of sensory details and unexpected observations consistently paint vivid pictures for the reader.

More Ideas

Looking for more ideas on using literature to teach the trait of ideas? We recommend *Books, Lessons, Ideas for Teaching the Six Traits: Writing at Middle and High School,* published by Great Source. Compiled and annotated by Vicki Spandel. For information, please phone 800-289-4490.

Draw on the Count of Three

For use with pages 7–11 in the Student Traitbook

In this lesson, students will learn the importance of prewriting strategies. The more prewriting strategies a writer has in his or her repertoire, the less likely that writer is going to waste a lot of time staring blankly into space or watching the blinking cursor on the monitor. Many writers use word webs or make lists. In this lesson, though, students will use two prewriting techniques they are less likely to have tried.

Objectives

Students will learn two specific prewriting strategies: sketching as a way of bringing out details they might not otherwise recall and using "detail bricks" to build strong images.

Skills Focus

- Practicing two prewriting strategies
- Recognizing the connection between prewriting and drafting
- Recognizing the connection between strong details and strong writing

Time Frame

Allow about 40 minutes for this lesson. It can be divided into two parts. Ask students to do the sketch for "Fun in the Great Outdoors" (20 minutes) as the first part of the lesson. In Part 2 of the lesson, ask students to create their own "stack of bricks" graphics and to begin a piece of writing related to that graphic (20 minutes).

Setting Up the Lesson

To introduce (or review) the trait of ideas, read Student Traitbook page 7 to students. Point out the bulleted list, which tells students what they will be working on in the next four lessons. Students may be unsure of the connections between drawing and writing. In addition, you need to assure them that this lesson is NOT about being a great artist. It's about using memories and impressions to capture details that might otherwise be lost. A good way to begin the lesson is to create a drawing of your own as a prewriting activity for a story or piece of writing. Don't worry about your artistic talents. If you cannot draw well, so much the better! Your basic drawing will build students' confidence that they can do this, too.

Good topics to match with a drawing activity include these (but please feel free to use one of your own):

• An unforgettable person

• A strange gift

• A favorite (or least favorite) pet

• Food no one could eat

Choose a topic, and do a very simple sketch on a blank overhead. Show it to your students, and ask them to tell you what the picture might inspire them to write about. Point out that your discussion, along with the drawing, brings out details you can use in your writing. Begin your writing as students offer suggestions.

Teaching the Lesson

Getting Off to an Energetic Start

Have students look at the questions on Student Traitbook pages 8–9. The purpose here is to show that thinking about a topic usually isn't enough. Something needs to be on the paper to guide the writing. One thing that helps is a sketch. Will everyone's sketch look a little different? We hope so!

Picture It in Your Head—Then, Draw It on Paper

Here's where students get to have some fun drawing. Remind them that this activity is just for fun; pictures will not be assessed in any way. Be sure students provide titles for their drawings. A title helps give direction to writing. These are the combined purposes of this opening activity: direction and detail. If students are willing, invite them to share their pictures in small groups (just as you shared yours earlier). They can ask questions of one another and predict what the writings will be about.

Labeling the Bricks (Another Prewriting Trick)

In this part of the lesson, students move from drawing pictures to creating a graphic organizer called detail bricks. To do this, they need to look closely at their pictures and pick out specific details they can put into words. For example, a sketch of a pet dog might lead to a detail brick with the words "shaggy fur." The graphic organizer on page 10 has six bricks. Point out that this does NOT mean you always need six. One writer might fill five, another eight. Your writers should keep going until they have enough details to "build" a good picture or story for the reader.

Build It for Your Readers

At this point, students should be working independently, using their drawings and graphic organizers to create original pieces of writing. Each "detail brick" should yield one or two sentences that add important information to a description, essay, or story. Thus, a student with four bricks in his or her graphic should have a fairly easy time constructing a four-sentence paragraph, or a slightly longer piece.

Share and Compare

Invite students to share their writings with one another in small groups. Remind them to help other writers see the connections they have made (or missed!) between their drawings/graphic organizers and the writing itself.

Extending the Lesson

- Share your own writing, and invite students to help you connect what you have written to your original drawing.
- Discuss with students the process of drawing as a form of prewriting: How difficult is it? How helpful is it? Did any students think of details they might have overlooked without the sketch?
- Picture to Picture: Is the picture created in the reader's mind likely to match the picture created by the writer as a form of prewriting? Why or why not?
- Ask students to use their imaginations to think like another writer. Read aloud a very short piece of informational writing from a brochure, newspaper, textbook, or how-to manual. Ask students to create drawings they think the writer might have used had he or she used this form of prewriting. Share drawings and discuss connections with the writing.

Narrowing Your Topic

For use with pages 12–15 in the Student Traitbook

In this lesson, students gain practice narrowing a large, unwieldy topic down to a manageable size.

Objectives

Students will understand that highly focused, well-defined topics do not create themselves. Writers must work to whittle a big topic down to the size that allows for focused, interesting writing.

Skills Focus

- Understanding the difference between a HUGE topic and a manageable topic
- Using your own inner navigator's questions to bring a big topic down to size
- Knowing when a topic is small enough so that a writer can begin writing

Time Frame

Allow about 30 minutes for this lesson, excluding *Extending the Lesson.*

Setting Up the Lesson

Talk about the difference between big topics and topics that are manageable—in other words, topics a writer could handle in a 2 to 5 page paper. Give students some examples of possible topics, and let them give you a thumbs-up/thumbs-down vote on manageable versus not manageable. Examples might include these:

- School (Not manageable yet!)

- The day my brother fell out of the tree (Manageable)

- History (Not manageable yet!)

- The courage of Harriet Tubman (Yes! Manageable!)

Now, see whether your students can take a topic from large and unwieldy to manageable. Toss out a very general topic like one of these:

- Music

- Movies

- Middle School

- Families

Ask student pairs to choose one of these topics and narrow the focus to make it more manageable. Do not worry about how they do it. This is just a warm-up. Do, however, discuss results. List the narrowed topics on the board or overhead, and ask students to share how they got there. Are the topics narrow enough? Discuss this with the class.

Teaching the Lesson

Listening to Your Inner Navigator

As drivers drive, they are forever asking and answering questions in their heads: *Which way do I go now? Do I turn here? Am I there yet?* Writers need to do basically the same thing. Use the driving example to help your student writers understand how to take advantage of the inner navigator inside a writer's head. Remind them that writers' questions typically start with the boldface words on page 13 of their Student Traitbook: **Who, What, When, Where, Why, How, Which,** and so on. They need some practice thinking of questions that begin with these key words.

Which Way to Topicville?

In this portion of the lesson, students have an opportunity to review an example of how writers can use questions to navigate their way to a narrow topic. In the example, the writer begins with a very large topic, *sports,* and winds up with something he or she can handle in a fairly short space: *tracing the history of lacrosse to its origin with Native Americans.*

Take a few minutes to discuss the example, making sure the process is clear to your students. What other questions might the writer have asked? Do your students think the topic is narrow enough at this point for the writer to begin writing? Most students should find it about right, but some may think it's still too big. That's fine. Ask how they could narrow it further to give it even more focus.

You're the Navigator, So You Ask the Questions

It is time for students to use what they have learned about forming good navigator's questions to steer themselves to "Topicville." Remind them that the idea here is to come up with a topic narrow enough that the writer feels comfortable writing about it. There is really no magical right answer to this. No sign appears to tell the writer, "You're there!" The writer must listen to the inner navigator. You may also wish to remind students that if a topic really is too big, it will show up in the writing; big topics are VERY hard to keep in focus.

Invite students to share their navigating results first in small groups and then with the class. Have students share their original topics, the questions they asked themselves, and their final topics. Who came up with the most focused, manageable topics? Be sure to share these with the class. Which questions were especially helpful? You may wish to list these.

Extending the Lesson

- Model the "road to Topicville" approach by asking students to give *you* a very big topic and then narrow the topic. Write your questions on the board or overhead as you go, and answer them aloud.

- Invite students to try writing the introductory paragraph based on the narrowed topic. Do they find it easy to get started?

- Choose one of the best examples of topic narrowing from your class. Then divide the class into two groups. Ask each student in the first group to write an introductory paragraph on the original topic— *before* it was narrowed down. Ask each student in the second group to write an introductory paragraph on the second topic, *after* it was narrowed down. Read some results aloud, and discuss the benefits of a narrow topic.

From Fuzzy to Focused

For use with pages 16–19 in the Student Traitbook

Fuzzy writing leaves readers bewildered—and often bored, as well. By transforming fuzzy writing into something understandable, writers not only make the reader's job a whole lot easier but also help guarantee that their message will not be lost or misunderstood.

Objectives

Students will learn specific techniques for making fuzzy writing clear and apply those techniques in revising a piece that lacks clarity.

Skills Focus

- Identifying specific words or phrases that contribute to detail
- Identifying strategies an author uses to make writing clear and precise
- Emulating those strategies in revising a piece of fuzzy writing to make it clear

Time Frame

Allow about 40 minutes for this lesson, excluding any extensions. You can divide the lesson into two parts if you wish. In Part 1 (20 minutes), ask students to analyze the passage by Pam Muñoz Ryan on pages 16–17 of the Student Traitbook and to complete the "Person, Place, Thing, Event" chart that accompanies this piece. In Part 2 (20 minutes), ask students to respond to the questions under "What Did the Author Do?" and to revise the "Fuzzy Writing" sample about the car breaking down on page 19 of the Student Traitbook.

Setting Up the Lesson

Fuzzy writing creates fuzzy pictures in a reader's mind. Discuss with students the example presented in the Lesson 3 Introduction on page 16 of the Student Traitbook. Did students have any idea what this writer was talking about from the first few lines? To make sure that students get the idea, let the class have some fun by creating fuzzy examples of their own. Ask them to write passages that are unclear, confusing, and vague. Have fun reading them aloud. If you like, have a "Fuzzy Writing Contest," and choose a winner—and some runners up as well!

Teaching the Lesson

Sharing an Example:
Esperanza Rising

You can read the sample from Pam Muñoz Ryan aloud, or ask one of your students to read it. (Allow a little time for silent reading/rehearsal if you do this.) It is important that the passage be read with expression. Ask students what they see, smell, hear, and feel as they listen. You may wish to give students a second time to read the passage silently on their own, looking for details they may have missed on the first reading. Encourage them to underline any important details or to make notes in the margins.

What Can You See?

Invite students to discuss with their partners the details they noticed. Then have them work individually or with a partner to complete the *Person, Place, Thing, Event* chart on page 17 of the Student Traitbook. They should come up with as many words and phrases as they can.

Share and Compare

Ask student pairs to share a few key words and phrases for each entry with other student pairs. Discuss results as a class. Did any student pair discover details that others missed?

What Did the Author Do?

In responding to the list, students should notice that virtually everything listed is missing from the shorter version. No wonder this "revised" version of Ryan's writing is so barren of detail. Point out that the things listed— e.g., clear, precise word choice or things I can picture in my mind—are actually specific features good writers include in their writing to make it clear. Your student writers can, and should, use them, too.

From Fuzzy to Focused in a Flash

This time, students begin with a piece of fuzzy writing and the challenge is to make it clear. They will have the opportunity to use what they have learned in analyzing the passage about the grapes to revise a weak piece of writing (about the car breaking down on the road). Students should work individually and then share with partners. They can also share ideas with the class. Discuss students' results. What specific techniques did your students use in going from fuzzy to focused?

Extending the Lesson

- Ask students to share their revisions of the the broken-down car paragraph with the class. Share your revision, too.

- Make a list of favorite words or phrases from the revisions. What works especially well? Why?

- Look back at the fuzzy language in the original piece. What specific words or phrases did students identify that make this piece weak? Ask them to look at a piece of their own writing. Can they identify any similar fuzzy words or phrases? Have them take time to revise those now.

- Have students analyze a random piece of writing from a textbook, encyclopedia, or a newspaper. What are students' responses? Is the piece fuzzy or focused? Could some words or phrases be improved? Which ones? Go ahead—revise!

That's Pretty Sketchy!

For use with pages 20–23 in the Student Traitbook

Detailed writing is interesting writing—and being interested is what keeps readers turning pages. Moreover, readers do not usually want to do *all* the work of making meaning from a text. If they want readers to "stay tuned," writers must make the reading enjoyable and informative, filling in details that hold a reader's attention.

Objectives

Students will gain experience analyzing the reader appeal of several pieces of writing and then select one piece to revise.

Skills Focus

- Understanding the power of details to keep readers "tuned in"
- Analyzing the reader appeal of selected pieces of writing
- Identifying the specific qualities that make one piece of writing more appealing than another
- Revising a weak piece of writing to increase its appeal

Time Frame

Allow about 35 minutes for this lesson, excluding any extensions.

Setting Up the Lesson

This is a lesson about "staying tuned" and interested. Ask students to think of a time when they drifted away and lost interest during a class, watching TV, or listening to a parent or sibling. Talk about what causes a person to stop paying attention and lose interest. List the things students mention. Now, connect those same qualities to writing. What makes readers lose interest? Perhaps your students will mention some of the following things:

- The writing is hard to understand.
- The writing has no details.
- The writing doesn't connect to anything in my own life.
- The writer sounds bored—or uninterested.
- The topic is not interesting.

Let students know they will now have a chance to analyze some pieces of writing to see how high the reader appeal of each piece is.

Teaching the Lesson

"Stay Tuned" or "Change Channels"

In this portion of the lesson, students will analyze three pieces: "My Dog," "All About My Brother," and "The Secret Woods." You should read each piece aloud as students follow along—then let them discuss that piece with a partner before going on to the next one. Be sure students also write their responses under the section marked *My Thoughts.* Those notes will be important to the closing writing activity for this lesson.

Most students should find *The Secret Woods* the most appealing of the three samples. It is detailed, suspenseful, and highly focused. The writer uses clues without telling too much and thereby makes us want to keep reading. The first two examples, by contrast, are both sketchy, though each contains the promise of a good story—if only the writers had noticed! In "My Dog," for example, we learn that despite many rules about pets, people in the apartment building have a variety of pets, including snakes and ferrets. How do they get by with it? In *All About My Brother,* the writer confesses he is responsible for the cast on Tanner's arm, but never explains how or why. You may wish to discuss these undeveloped potential stories with your students.

Take time to discuss students' responses to each piece. Continue until you feel your class has a good sense of what makes one piece work better than another.

Time to Revise

Ask students to choose one of the weaker pieces (they should be choosing *My Dog or All About My Brother*) and revise it, making it more detailed and interesting. Let them know that they can invent details as they need to—so long as they do not wander from the writer's original story. They can also leave out anything they feel is unneeded. Remind students that the idea is to keep the audience "tuned in." Be sure to read revisions aloud and discuss them.

Extending the Lesson

- List the strategies the author of "The Secret Woods" used to make the story interesting. How do the strategies compare with those your student writers used in their revisions?

- Ask students to work with partners to do one more round of revision. In part 1 of this activity, each writer should create a three to four sentence paragraph that is very sketchy. Have partners trade paragraphs and revise. When students have finished, ask them to read the results. Did they bring their partner's writing to life? Would an audience stay tuned? Read results to the whole class and see what their response is.

- Have students create a dull, uninteresting piece for you to revise. Revise it in front of the class, and talk about the strategies you are using as you revise.

Ideas

Teacher's Guide pages 5, 120–131
Transparency numbers 1–4

Objective

Students will review and apply what they have learned about the trait of ideas.

Reviewing Ideas

Review with students what they have learned about the trait of ideas. Ask students to discuss what ideas are and to explain why ideas are important in a piece of writing. Then ask them to recall the main points about ideas that are discussed in Unit 1. Students' responses should include the following points:

- Use prewriting strategies to plan your writing.
- Narrow big topics down to manageable size.
- Transform fuzzy writing into focused writing.
- Write in order to keep your readers "tuned in."

Applying Ideas

To help students apply what they have learned about ideas, distribute copies of the Student Rubric for Ideas on page 5 of this Teacher's Guide. Students will use these to score one or more of the sample papers that begin on page 116. The papers for ideas are also on overhead transparencies 1–4.

Before students score the papers, explain that a rubric is a grading system to determine the score a piece of writing should receive for a particular trait. Preview the Student Rubric for Ideas, pointing out that a paper very strong in ideas receives a score of 6 and a paper very weak in ideas receives a score of 1. Tell students to read the rubric and then read the paper to be scored. Then tell them to look at the paper and rubric together to determine the score the paper should receive. Encourage students to make notes on each paper to help them score it. For example, they might put a check mark next to an interesting detail or draw a line through unnecessary information.

Overview

This unit focuses on organization—putting information in an order that makes sense and that both entertains and enlightens a reader. Lessons in this unit build on the skills from Unit 1, since strong organization helps showcase ideas, making key ideas stand out.

The focus of the instruction in this unit will be

- helping students identify organizational patterns.
- giving students practice in matching an organizational pattern to a writing task.
- showing students how to build word bridges through skillful use of transitions.
- giving students an opportunity to put their organizational skills together in one orderly paragraph.

Organization: A Definition

Organization is about the logical and effective presentation of key ideas and details. Good organization holds a piece of writing together and makes it easy to follow—like good instructions or a clear road map. Several things make organization work well: an organizational pattern that makes sense and matches the purpose for the writing, strong transitions that link the writer's ideas together, a compelling lead that pulls the reader in, and an appropriate conclusion that effectively wraps things up.

The Unit at a Glance

The following lessons in the Teacher's Guide and practice exercises in the Student Traitbook will help develop understanding of the trait of organization. The Unit Summary provides an opportunity to practice evaluating papers for organization.

Unit Introduction: Organization

Teacher's Guide pages 20–24

The unique features of organization are presented along with rubrics and a list of recommended literature for teaching organization.

Lesson 5: Name That Pattern!

Teacher's Guide pages 25–27
Student Traitbook pages 24–28

Students are introduced to five organizational patterns and gain practice in recognizing those patterns in samples of writing.

Lesson 6: The Right Tool for the Job

Teacher's Guide pages 28–30
Student Traitbook pages 29–32

Lesson 6 builds on Lesson 5 by giving students an opportunity to match an organizational pattern to a task and then imitating one pattern in an original piece of writing.

Lesson 7: Building Bridges: Connecting Ideas

Teacher's Guide pages 31–33
Student Traitbook pages 33–36

Writing that lacks strong transitions can be very hard to follow; the reader must make all the connections. In this lesson, students learn to identify good transitions, applying them in their own writing.

Lesson 8: Putting It All Together

Teacher's Guide pages 34–36
Student Traitbook pages 37–40

Athletes must eventually put together all the skills they've practiced and play a real game. Lesson 8 gives students a chance to do just that by applying a range of organizational skills in creating a paragraph about the coral snake.

Unit Summary: Organization

Teacher's Guide page 37
Overhead numbers 5–8

Use the student rubric on page 23 and the activities in the Summary to practice assessing writing for the trait of organization. Remember, 5-point rubrics, along with rationales for scores on sample papers, appear in the Appendix of this Teacher's Guide, pages 192–214.

Teacher Rubric for Organization

6
- The writer focuses on the main message throughout the paper.
- The organizational pattern is a great fit for the topic, purpose, and audience; it enhances the reader's understanding of the text.
- Transitions are smooth, clearly connecting sentences and ideas.
- The lead is strong and compelling, and the conclusion is thoroughly satisfying.

5
- The writer seldom wanders from the main point.
- The organizational pattern fits the topic, purpose, and audience.
- Transitions adequately connect ideas.
- The lead is appealing, and the conclusion works.

4
- The writer wanders briefly from the main point, but it is not distracting or confusing.
- The organizational pattern works well in most places.
- Transitions are present, but the reader has to make *some* connections.
- The lead and conclusion are functional if not original.

3
- The writer wanders from the main point enough to create some confusion.
- The organizational pattern may not match the task well; it may be too formulaic or simply hard to follow.
- Transitions are sometimes present, sometimes not.
- The lead and conclusion are present; one or both need work.

2
- Lack of order frequently leaves the reader feeling lost.
- The pattern is so formulaic that it's distracting—or there is no pattern.
- Transitions are rarely attempted.
- The lead and conclusion are either missing or need a lot of work.

1
- The text is basically a disjointed collection of random thoughts.
- There is no identifiable organizational pattern. It's impossible to follow.
- Transitions are absent. Ideas do not seem connected.
- There is no real lead or conclusion.

Student Rubric for Organization

6
- I stick with one topic. I never wander.
- I chose an organizational pattern that fits my topic, purpose, and audience very well. This pattern helps make my meaning clear.
- My transitions build strong bridges from sentence to sentence, from idea to idea.
- My lead will grab the reader's attention, and my conclusion is great.

5
- I stick with one topic most of the time.
- My organizational pattern fits my topic, purpose, and audience.
- Most of my transitions work.
- My lead introduces the reader to the paper, and my conclusion wraps up main points effectively.

4
- I might have wandered a *little* from my main topic—but I got back on track.
- I have an organizational pattern. I think it fits the task OK.
- I used some transitions, but the reader needs to make some connections.
- My lead goes with the rest of my paper, and my conclusion lets the reader know the paper is finished.

3
- I wandered from my main topic now and then.
- I tried to follow an organizational pattern. I'm not sure it fits my purpose.
- I thought about transitions, but the reader needs to make a lot of connections.
- I have a lead and a conclusion, but they both need work.

2
- I wrote about too many things. I forgot what my main topic was.
- I do not think there is a pattern here. This is more like a messy closet!
- I might have one or two transitions, but I'm not sure they connect things clearly.
- I think I forgot to write a lead, and I think I forgot my conclusion, too. Maybe I wrote "The End" . . .

1
- This doesn't make any sense. I don't even *have* a main topic yet.
- Pattern? Are you kidding? Nothing goes with anything else.
- How could I have transitions when nothing goes with anything else?
- There is no lead or conclusion.

Recommended Books for Teaching Organization

Use excerpts from these books or from your favorites to model organizational structures, transitions, leads, and conclusions.

Collard, Sneed B. III. 2000. *Lizard Island: Science and Scientists on Australia's Great Barrier Reef.* New York: Franklin Watts. Masterful interweaving of narrative and pure informational writing describing biologists at the Lizard Island Research Station. Look closely at leads and titles—highly original.

Fleischman, Paul. 1995. *Bull Run.* New York: HarperCollins. The Civil War from multiple perspectives. Voices rotate throughout the chapters, giving this book a strong and fun-to-imitate organizational structure.

Kimball, Violet T. 2000. *Stories of Young Pioneers: In Their Own Words.* Missoula, MT: Mountain Press. Ideal model for using journals as an organizational structure.

Paulsen, Gary. 1998. *My Life in Dog Years.* New York: Bantam Books. Shows a simple organizational structure that's still original: an autobiography organized according to dogs that Paulsen has known and loved.

St. George, Judith. 2000. *So You Want to Be President?* New York: Penguin Putnam. Quirky, imaginative approach to organizing information on the presidents—NOT president by president, as in the usual clichéd approach!

Schwartz, David M. 2001. *Q Is for Quark: A Science Alphabet Book.* Berkely: Tricycle Press. Original, captivating leads and conclusions throughout the book. Excellent transitions. (Great for voice, too!)

Sachar, Louis. 1998. *Holes.* New York: Farrar, Straus & Giroux. The first chapter raises numerous questions. Use it to make predictions.

Sebranek, Patrick, Dave Kemper and Verne Meyer. 1999. *Write Source 2000.* Wilmington, MA: Great Source Education Group, Inc. User-friendly approaches to organizing information, keeping things in focus, writing leads and conclusions, using transitions wisely, and much more.

More Ideas

Looking for more ideas on using literature to teach the trait of organization? We recommend *Books, Lessons, Ideas for Teaching the Six Traits: Writing at Middle and High School,* published by Great Source. Compiled and annotated by Vicki Spandel. For information, please phone 800-289-4490.

Lesson 5

Name That Pattern!

For use with pages 25–28 in the Student Traitbook

The most intriguing details in the world can be lost on a reader if those details are not organized—rather like that one special treasure lost in the clutter of a disorganized garage sale. Patterns help readers follow informational trails. It takes hard work to organize writing well. But it's one important way of ensuring that no informational treasures are overlooked.

Objectives

Students will learn five patterns for organizing writing and will gain practice in identifying those patterns in selected samples.

Skills Focus

- Understanding the importance of organizing information
- Recognizing and understanding five organizational patterns
- Identifying patterns in written samples
- Creating a piece of original writing imitating one of the five patterns introduced in the lesson

Time Frame

Allow about 45 minutes for this lesson. It can be divided into two parts. Ask students to review the passage from *The Secret Shortcut*, to read through and discuss the list under "Five Organizational Patterns," and to identify the patterns in samples 1–5 under "Name That Pattern" (25 minutes). In the second part of the lesson, ask students to write an original paragraph imitating one of the patterns identified in this lesson (20 minutes).

Setting Up the Lesson

Looking for organizational patterns in a piece of writing can be a challenging task. Start with a simple example, such as a recipe. First, read the instructions out of order—then ask students how many feel ready to prepare the dish! Next, show students how a recipe is organized: a list of ingredients followed by step-by-step instructions. This pattern shows the reader exactly what is needed and how to put it all together:

You may wish to share other examples in which the pattern is very clear. How-to books and manuals that follow a step-by-step order are good for this. Newspaper articles usually follow a clear pattern of organization also: the lead gives who, what, where, when, and how information; the body of details relays whatever is currently known; and a conclusion states what information still needs to be gathered or what is likely to occur next. As you share these warm-up examples, ask students to describe the patterns.

Teaching the Lesson

Five Organizational Patterns

The five patterns listed and defined here are common in writing and should be easy for most students to imitate as well. Let students read the list first, identifying those patterns they have used in their own writing. Then, as you discuss the list with the class, take time to ask how many have used each pattern. You may also wish to ask students to identify specific things they have read that fit each pattern.

Name That Pattern!

Here, students must read closely and carefully, looking for clues that show which pattern of organization the writer is using in each of the samples. Students should work independently on this task and then share with a partner before discussing their findings with the class. Here are the patterns in the five samples:

Sample 1
Cause and Effect
The cause here is the attack; the result is beefed-up security, with longer lines, more checkpoints, and some business closures.

Sample 2
Order of Location
Sometimes this pattern is called visual or spatial organization. The writer paints a picture by directing attention to the steep trail, trees and hills, ocean, steep drop-off, jagged rocks, and so on.

Sample 3

Chronological Order

The giveaway here is the writer's sharing of the time of day. We follow the writer from 6 A.M. to noon, with details of activities at regular intervals.

Invite students to share their conclusions on various patterns with a partner and then with the class as a whole. You may find some disagreement—though the patterns are clear enough that a good case can be made for how each piece is organized. Extend the discussion until all (or most) students feel comfortable.

Imitating a Pattern

For this part of the lesson, students should work alone, writing a paragraph that imitates one of the five patterns you have discussed as a class. Students should feel free to select a personal topic, but several are given as suggestions. The suggested topics are designed to fit various patterns of organization.

Extending the Lesson

- Share a paragraph of your own writing, and invite students to identify the pattern you have used.

- Have each student work with a partner to find examples of each organizational pattern. (Each team of students should look for one or two samples.) Read a few aloud to see whether students can identify the patterns they hear. Post examples, too, for students to study.

- Now that students have had practice imitating one organizational pattern, ask them to try another. The more organizational patterns students attempt, the more clearly they will fix these patterns in their minds.

The Right Tool for the Job

For use with pages 29–32 in the Student Traitbook

In this lesson, students will review the five organizational patterns introduced in Lesson 5 and then add two more to their repertoire.

Objectives

Students will understand that they can organize information in many ways. Skillful writers try to match each writing task to an organizational pattern, making the writing easy for a reader to follow.

Skills Focus

- Understanding seven different forms of organization
- Recognizing that good organization depends on the writer's task and purpose
- Matching a specific writing task with the organizational pattern that fits it best

Time Frame

Allow about 35 minutes for this lesson, excluding *Extending the Lesson.*

Setting Up the Lesson

Use some real-world examples to help students understand the concept of matching organizational structure to a task. For example, consider the organization of food within a refrigerator. Imagine that you have just bought two sacks of groceries and need to arrange them. Would alphabetical order work? Apples on the top shelf, zucchini on the bottom. Would this be a good arrangement? Most students should say no! So—ask them what *would* work. Suppose people come to a big clearance sale and have to line up at the cash register by date of birth— people with January birth dates first, people with December birth dates last. Would customers consider this approach logical? Could you arrange items in a grocery store by color? Everything green in Aisle 1, red items in Aisle 2, and so on? How do you decide on an organizational order for *anything?* What you want students to see is that organization *has* to fit the task to work well.

Teaching the Lesson

Seven Patterns: The Right Tools to Organize Your Writing

Students should be familiar with the first five patterns listed here. You may wish to review by asking them to describe each pattern without looking at the list in the Student Traitbook.

They can then read through the list one more time just to be sure they have those five patterns down. Finally, read through and discuss the two new forms of organization: step-by-step and main idea plus support. As in the previous lesson, ask students whether they can come up with their own writing examples (in or out of school) that reflect each type of organization.

Match Them Up!

In this portion of the lesson, students will match writing tasks with one of the organizational patterns on the list they have just looked at. Although you may think there is a "best" way to organize each piece of writing, it is quite possible that students will come up with more than one approach that works. Here are the suggested approaches:

Description of a favorite painting
Order of location (spatial) OR *Main idea and support*

Diary of your week at Outdoor School
Chronological

Opinion paper on why the school day should be lengthened
Cause and effect (problem/solution) OR *Order of importance*

Campaign speech
Main idea and support OR *Order of importance* OR *Comparison (comparing two candidates)*

Newspaper story on vandalizing
Cause and effect OR *Main idea and support* OR *Chronological order* (how events unfolded)

Article on snowboarding versus skiing
Comparison

Explanation of the connection between lunch prices and school budget
Cause and effect
Order of importance

Share and Compare

Students should share first with a partner and then with the class. Be sure to leave room for more than one organizational approach per task, but ask your students to explain just how an organizational approach would work. Their explanations should take this general form: "I would begin with information on _____. Then I would include _____. I would wrap up my paper with _____." The purpose here is to increase students' organizational skills by requiring them to do some mental planning.

Putting a Pattern to Use

Here students start with a particular topic and choose a pattern that matches it. Keep in mind that students can approach this topic (a favorite season) in a number of ways. A student could write a diary, reflecting on events of the season (chronological); give specific reasons for choosing that season (most to least important); describe it (spatial);

compare it with another season (comparison); and so on. In short, the topic does not *dictate* the organizational approach, so encourage your students to be creative in determining how they will organize their writing.

Extending the Lesson

- Ask students to share their "favorite season" writings in response groups and with the class. Notice the various patterns of organization reflected in their writing, and list the different approaches your students have taken. Talk about how many different ways there are to organize a piece of writing.

- Look at any piece of writing (from any content area) that your students are currently studying. Ask them to brainstorm other ways the same information *could* have been organized. Did the writer choose the most effective way?

- As in Lesson 5, invite students to examine another piece of writing, this time imitating another organizational pattern. They may wish to try organizing the "favorite season" information in another way—or choose a new topic altogether.

Lesson 7
Building Bridges: Connecting Ideas

For use with pages 33–36 in the Student Traitbook

Writing that's transition-free is very difficult to navigate. Readers may find themselves saying, "How in the *world* did we get to a discussion of baseball? I thought this was an article on poisonous frogs!" Strong writers use transitions to link sentences or key thoughts together, building word bridges from point to point, so that writing is easy to follow: "Stan thought he would become a pitcher. However, the first time he saw a poisonous frog up close, he knew he'd be a biologist."

Objectives

Students will learn the value of transitions and gain practice in identifying transitional phrases and using them in their own writing.

Skills Focus

- Understanding the concept of "transition"
- Identifying transitional words or phrases in a piece of writing
- Revising a piece with weak or missing transitions to make those transitions stronger

Time Frame

Allow about 40 minutes for this lesson, excluding any extensions. You can divide the lesson into two parts if you wish. In part 1 (20 minutes), ask students to analyze the passage by Robin Cody on page 34 of the Student Traitbook, paying particular attention to the highlighted transitional words. Also have students identify the transitional words or phrases in the passage by Jack Gantos on page 35 of the Traitbook. In part 2 of the lesson (20 minutes), give students an opportunity to be bridge builders themselves by revising the sample paragraph on page 36 of the Traitbook under "You Build the Bridges."

Setting Up the Lesson

Students need to understand what a transition is in order to use transitional phrases effectively. You can illustrate this quite simply by putting two seemingly unrelated sentences on the overhead, and inviting students to "build a bridge" by supplying a transitional word or phrase.

Example:

Jack refused to wear his new hat. It was snowing.

Even though *it was snowing, Jack refused to wear his new hat.*

Teaching the Lesson

Sharing an Example:
Voyage of a Summer Sun

Read aloud the passage from Robin Cody's book *Voyage of a Summer Sun.* Ask students to both look and listen for transitional phrases as you read. Since these are printed in color, they should be easy to spot—but the idea is to reinforce students' understanding of how transitions connect ideas.

After talking through the *Voyage of a Summer Sun* passage, look carefully at the list of transitional words from *Write Source 2000.* Give students some time to study this list, and ask how many of them use these words as transitions in their own writing. Also explain that this list does not represent all possible transitions. Writers sometimes use pronouns as transitions, for example: *Sheila did not like visiting the dentist.* **It** *was her least favorite activity!* In this example, **It** refers to visiting the dentist; this word connects the two sentences. Reinforce the idea that a transition is any word or group of words that builds a bridge between sentences or ideas.

Some More Practice

This time around, students must spot the transitions for themselves. Read the passage from *Jack on the Tracks* aloud if you think this will be helpful to your students. If you think that students can find the transitions, let them read the passage on their own. Students should work with partners on this activity and should fill out the brief chart under "Share and Compare" prior to any class discussion.

The following is a copy of the passage with transitional phrases underlined.

Jack Gantos, *Jack on the Tracks: Four Seasons of Fifth Grade.* (New York: Farrar, Straus & Giroux, 2001), p. 41

While I was thinking about the mysterious differences between boys and girls, Mrs. Pierre turned her back toward us and faced the blackboard. Above the alphabet letters on top of the board she had mounted a rearview mirror from a car so she could keep her eyes on us even as she wrote, and <u>when she did write</u>, <u>it</u> was amazing. She put a piece of chalk in each hand and stretched them out as far as she could. <u>Then she started writing</u> with both hands at the same time. <u>Her left hand</u> wrote normally from the beginning of the sentence to the right. Her right hand was incredible. She started with the period of the sentence, <u>and then</u> with the last letter of the last word, and continued to write completely backward from right to left. She did <u>this</u> with ease, and she did <u>it</u> all in cursive, and she finished the sentence exactly in the middle where her two hands met and seamlessly completed the final word.

Share and Compare

Ask student pairs to share with each other first, completing the checklist to show how many transitions each student found.

You Build the Bridges

This passage about a snow day suffers from weak, missing, or inappropriate transitions. It needs help! Be sure students read through the passage once to get the general idea. Then suggest that they read it a second time, inserting transitional words or replacing those that do not work. The following is a *suggested* revision.

The news report said there could be snow in the morning. **Consequently,**

I found my boots, gloves, and hat. **Later** I ran upstairs to tell my sisters the good news. **When I got around to it,** I told my brother the good news also. He was pretty excited about the possibility of having a day off from school. My sisters were pretty happy about it **also.** My mom was the only one who didn't think a snow day would be fun. **You see,** she would be the only one who wouldn't get a real day off. **For that reason,** we kept our celebration to ourselves.

Extending the Lesson

- Share your own revision of the snow day paper. You may come up with transitions no one else thought of.

- Have students work in groups to design "transition quizzes." Each group will write a short paragraph that has no transitions, weak transitions, or the wrong transitions. HINT: It helps to write the paragraph WITH transitions first and then recopy it with the weak transition challenges in place.

Putting It All Together

For use with pages 37–40 in the Student Traitbook

Eventually, students need to put all the pieces together to create a well-organized piece of writing. This means crafting a compelling lead, putting information in an order that makes sense, eliminating unneeded information, using strong transitions to link ideas, and wrapping it all up with a good conclusion.

Objectives

Students will work from start to finish on a paragraph to create a piece with exemplary organization—one so strong it could be used to teach the trait!

Skills Focus

- Selecting quality details from a list
- Selecting a main topic by analyzing how details work together
- Choosing an organizational pattern to fit the topic
- Writing a strong lead
- Putting details in an order that makes sense
- Writing a strong conclusion
- Analyzing personal writing for its strengths/problems in organization

Time Frame

Allow about 45 minutes for this lesson, excluding any extensions.

Setting Up the Lesson

This is a lesson about putting all the organizational strategies together. Ask students to list the keys to strong organization. (Have them do this without looking at their rubrics if they can.) Then have them list things that can go wrong with organization. Post both lists so that students can refer to them throughout the lesson. If you wish, share a piece of writing, and ask students to comment on the strengths or problems in organization.

Teaching the Lesson

Keep, Toss, and Narrow

As students push their mental "shopping carts" through the list of details on coral snakes, encourage them to look for what is most interesting or important. They should eliminate *everything* that is general, redundant, or common knowledge. Most students should find that they have a remaining list of about eight details. They should work individually, for they may not all agree on what is most important or interesting.

What's the Big Idea?

This may seem like a small step, but it's very important. Organization depends on focus—and focus depends on having a main idea or main message to convey. Students should look carefully at their lists of remaining details (the ones that went into the cart) and see whether they suggest a main message. Here's one example based on the list: *Though coral snakes are venomous, they are not usually dangerous to humans.* Once a writer has a main idea, it is easier to put the remaining details in an order that makes sense.

Ready to Write?

Here is an opportunity for students to choose an organizational pattern that fits the main idea of the paper. Encourage students to look at the lists of organizational patterns from Lessons 5 and 6 to remind themselves of possibilities.

Off to a Good Start—the Toss-Up

When writing a strong lead, it's often helpful to look for the most interesting or startling piece of information from a list of details. Perhaps detail 2 (the bite of the coral snake can be deadly to humans) or detail 10 (if you try to hold a coral snake, it will try to bite) offers a good starting point. Interesting or unusual information is the stuff of a good lead. But leads can also involve anecdotes, quotations, or descriptions. You may wish to remind students of some of the best ways to begin an informational piece. Then see what leads they can come up with.

Keep the Game Going

Students can use the leads they wrote in the "Toss-Up" practice (immediately preceding) or come up with new ones. They should focus on having a strong lead, putting details into an order or pattern that makes sense, using good transitions, and closing with a strong conclusion.

Share Your Paragraph

As students share paragraphs, encourage listeners to pay attention to the short checklist on page 40 of the Student Traitbook and to offer feedback based on that list.

Extending the Lesson

- Wait two days, and then ask students to revise their paragraphs on the coral snake to make them even stronger in the trait of organization. Suggest some of the strategies writers use to revise, such as writing a stronger lead, changing the main idea, using a different organizational pattern, taking out unnecessary information, changing the conclusion, and using stronger transitions.

- Spend time discussing titles, encouraging students to come up with good titles for the pieces they have written. Explain that a good title, like a strong lead, gives the reader a sense of direction. Share titles.

- Read aloud your own paragraph on the coral snake. Invite students to assess it for the trait of organization. Does it have all the essentials in place? What did you think was YOUR main organizational strength? Did your students agree?

- Invite students to create a weak organizational piece for YOU to revise on the overhead. The rules are that the piece can have up to three organizational problems. Then see what you can do to improve it as students watch. Talk through your revisional steps as you complete them. (HINT: To make your task a little easier, the weak samples students give you should be no more than seven or eight sentences long. They should be double-spaced and printed or typed.)

Organization

Teacher's Guide pages 23, 132–143
Transparency numbers 5–8

Objective

Students will review and apply what they have learned about the trait of organization.

Reviewing Organization

Review with students what they have learned about the trait of organization. Ask students to discuss what organization means and to explain why it is important in a piece of writing. Then ask them to recall the main points about organization that are discussed in Unit 2. Students' responses should include the following points:

- Become familiar with organizational patterns.
- Put information in an order that makes sense.
- Use logical transitions.
- Begin with an interesting lead and write a strong conclusion.

Applying Organization

To help students apply what they have learned about the trait of organization, distribute copies of the Student Rubric for Organization on page 23 of this Teacher's Guide. Students will use these to score one or more of the sample papers that begin on page 116. The papers for organization are also on overhead transparencies 5–8.

Before students score the papers, explain that a rubric is a grading system to determine the score a piece of writing should receive for a particular trait. Preview the Student Rubric for Organization, pointing out that a paper that is well organized receives a score of 6 and a paper that is not organized receives a score of 1. Tell students to read the rubric and then read the paper to be scored. Then tell them to look at the paper and rubric together to determine the score the paper should receive. Encourage students to make notes on each paper to help them score it. For example, they might put a check mark next to a strong lead or conclusion and an X next to a weak lead or conclusion.

Overview

This unit focuses on voice, an intriguing trait that is a skillful blend of detail, enthusiasm, topic knowledge, audience awareness, and a writer's personality. As students explore samples of narrative and expository writing, they will have an opportunity to consider the importance of voice in capturing and holding a reader's attention.

The focus of the instruction in this unit will be

- helping students define the trait of voice in their own words
- encouraging students to consider how voice shifts with purpose and mode—for example, from narrative to expository writing
- showing students how to temper voice to match the needs of an audience
- inviting students to revise flat, voiceless writing by enriching the detail, adding dialogue, or using other writers' strategies

Voice: *A Definition*

As one teacher put it, your ideas are what you have to say; your voice is how you say it. Students and teachers often worry that voice cannot be taught because it is so closely linked to personality. Voice is much more than personality, however. It is also the skillful use of detail that enriches a passage and helps readers make personal connections. It is the writer's concern for the audience; voice changes as audience changes so that the voice in a business letter is not the voice in an impassioned personal narrative. Voice is also a reflection of confidence—confidence that can come only from knowing a topic well.

The Unit at a Glance

The following lessons in the Teacher's Guide and practice exercises in the Student Traitbook will help develop understanding of voice. The Unit Summary provides an opportunity to practice evaluating papers for voice.

Unit Overview: Voice

Teacher's Guide pages 38–42

The unique features of the trait of voice are presented along with rubrics and a list of recommended literature for teaching voice.

Lesson 9: Defining Voice in Your Own Words

Teacher's Guide pages 43–45
Student Traitbook pages 42–45

In this lesson, students identify voice in various samples and then create a personal definition.

Lesson 10: Voice in Expository Writing

Teacher's Guide pages 46–48
Student Traitbook pages 46–49

Students discover that even in expository writing, voice gives life to the writing; in this case, the voice comes from the writer's knowledge of and enthusiasm for the topic.

Lesson 11: "Hello, How Are You?" or "Waz Up?"

Teacher's Guide pages 49–51
Student Traitbook pages 50–53

When it comes to finding the appropriate voice for the occasion, audience is everything. We do not speak to friends or presidents of corporations in the same way; in this lesson, students learn that voice needs flexibility.

Lesson 12: From Flat to Fantastic

Teacher's Guide pages 52–54
Student Traitbook pages 54–57

What we see and feel as we read adds to *voice*. Students use detail that taps into images and feelings to transform a flat piece of writing into something appealing and reader-friendly.

Unit Summary: Voice

Teacher's Guide page 55
Overhead numbers 9–12

Use the student rubric on page 41 and the activities in the Summary to practice assessing writing for the trait of voice. Remember, 5-point rubrics, along with rationales for scores on sample papers, appear in the Appendix of this Teacher's Guide, pages 192–214.

Teacher Rubric for Voice

6
- This writing is as individual as fingerprints. If you know the writer, you can identify him or her readily.
- The reader will feel compelled to share the piece aloud.
- This writing is lively, energetic, and hard to put down. It explodes with energy.
- The voice is carefully selected to fit the purpose and audience perfectly.

5
- This paper stands out from others. The voice is recognizable if you know the writer.
- The reader would likely share this piece aloud.
- This writing shows strong feelings and is appealing to read. It has a lot of energy.
- The voice is suitable for the audience and purpose.

4
- This voice is distinctive though not unique.
- The reader might share parts of this piece aloud.
- Moments of passion, energy, or strong feelings are evident throughout.
- The voice is acceptable for the audience and purpose but could use refining.

3
- This is a functional, sincere voice, though not especially distinctive.
- The piece does not seem quite ready to be shared aloud.
- Moments of passion, energy, or strong feelings are rare. The reader needs to look for them.
- The voice may or may not seem acceptable for the purpose or audience.

2
- The voice is sometimes difficult to identify and is not distinctive.
- The piece is definitely not ready to share aloud.
- This writing could use a serious energy boost. The writer sounds bored.
- The voice is not a good match for audience and purpose.

1
- This voice is difficult to identify or describe, or it's the *wrong* voice for the writing task.
- Lack of voice makes this a piece the reader would *not* share aloud.
- No energy or excitement about the topic comes through.
- The voice is missing or wholly inappropriate for the audience and purpose.

Student Rubric for Voice

6
- This paper is so distinctive; the reader can tell at once that it's MY voice.
- I think the reader will definitely want to share this paper aloud.
- I LOVE this topic, and my enthusiasm will make the reader like it also.
- I thought of the needs and interests of my audience throughout the paper.
- The voice of this piece is perfect for my purpose.

5
- This voice stands out from others. It's personal.
- The reader might want to share this paper aloud—I would.
- I like this topic, so a lot of energy comes through.
- I considered my audience, and I think this voice is right.
- The voice is just right for my purpose.

4
- My voice comes through clearly in parts.
- The reader might share moments here and there.
- I like this topic for the most part. The writing has *some* energy.
- I think the voice is an OK match for my audience.
- My voice seems OK for my purpose.

3
- I am not sure whether this paper sounds like me or not.
- This paper isn't quite ready to share aloud yet.
- I could not get too excited about this topic.
- I was writing to get done, not writing for an audience.
- I do not know whether this voice fits my purpose.

2
- I do not think this sounds much like me.
- This paper is NOT ready to share aloud. There isn't enough voice!
- I did not like this topic. I think I sound a little bored or tired.
- I just wanted it to be over. I don't care whether anyone reads this.
- Since I am not sure what my purpose is, I don't know whether my voice fits or not.

1
- I do not hear any voice in this writing.
- Share this aloud? Not for anything!
- This topic was so-o-o-o boring—plus I didn't know much about it!
- Why would anyone want to read this? I don't even like it myself.
- I do not know what my purpose for writing this is.

Recommended Books for Teaching Voice

Share a whole book, a chapter, a strategy, or a favorite passage. Read as you'd like to hear your students read—with expression and life. Ask students questions like these: *How would you describe this voice? Who is the audience for this writing? How do you know? What strategies does this writer use to put voice into his or her writing?*

Claggett, Fran, Louann Reid, and Ruth Vinz. 1999. *Daybook of Critical Reading and Writing, Grade 6.* Wilmington, MA: Great Source Education Group, Inc. Outstanding excerpts from the best of modern literature combine with challenging writing tasks.

Creech, Sharon. 2001. *Love That Dog.* New York: Joanna Cotler Books. Through a poetic journal, the distinctive voice of Jack, a student, brings his story and his teacher (who never speaks directly) to life.

Creech, Sharon. 2000. *The Wanderer.* New York: HarperCollins. Vibrant voice, and an excellent example of how to show differing perspectives through multiple characters.

Dahl, Roald. 2002. *Danny the Champion of the World.* New York: Alfred A. Knopf, Inc. Dahl's comic genius is suspended momentarily in favor of a gentler, more philosophical tone. Notice the dialogue and descriptive passages.

Fleischman, Paul. 1997. *Seedfolks.* New York: HarperCollins. An array of voices perfect for read-alouds. Students can listen to shifts in tone and texture, and ask how Fleischman manages to capture so many (13!) totally different voices.

Fritz, Jean. 1995. *You Want Women to Vote, Lizzie Stanton?* New York: GP Putnam's Sons. A fine example of engaging voice in informational writing.

Sebranek, Patrick, Dave Kemper, and Verne Meyer. *Write Source 2000.* 1999. Wilmington, MA: Great Source Education Group, Inc. Information on revising for voice, creating an engaging voice, creating personal writing, making persuasive writing effective, achieving the right tone for the purpose, and connecting with an audience.

Spinelli, Jerry. 1997. *The Library Card.* New York: Scholastic, Inc. Spinelli's highly distinctive voice coupled with excellent organization.

More Ideas

Looking for more ideas on using literature to teach the trait of ideas? We recommend *Books, Lessons, Ideas for Teaching the Six Traits: Writing at Middle and High School,* published by Great Source. Compiled and annotated by Vicki Spandel. For information, please phone 800-289-4490.

Defining Voice in Your Own Words

For use with pages 41–45 in the Student Traitbook

Voice keeps readers interested and reading. It's an important trait to master for any writer who wants his or her message to be heard. This unit offers students an opportunity to explore a wide range of voices and deepen their understanding of how voice changes to fit audience and purpose.

Objectives

Students will respond to several different voices and develop a personal definition of voice.

Skills Focus

- Listening for voice
- Describing different voices
- Developing a personal definition of voice

Time Frame

Allow about 35 minutes for this lesson. The greatest amount of time should be devoted to reading the samples aloud and discussing what students hear. Some time must also be allowed for sharing reflections after students write their personal definitions of voice.

Setting Up the Lesson

Use the introduction on Student Traitbook page 41 to introduce (or review) and discuss the trait of voice. Point out the bulleted list that tells students what they will learn in the next four lessons. In this lesson, students will be listening for voice. It is helpful for them to hear a strong example and a weak example—perhaps based on the same passage. A good example to use for this exercise is the introduction to Roald Dahl's classic book *The Twits*. Start with a weak-voiced revision that might go something like this: *There were two people. Their names were Mr. and Mrs. Twit. They were not very nice to each other. They played mean tricks on each other. It was quite unpleasant.*

Now, read a portion of the actual introduction. (Choose a few passages to illustrate your point.) Ask students to comment briefly on the differences. Be sure students understand the *main* difference: While Dahl's original rings with voice, the "revised" version has virtually no voice at all. (Feel free, of course, to use any text you wish for this example. Be sure your revised version is as voice-free as you can make it.)

Teaching the Lesson

Voices on Parade

The instructions for this portion of the lesson call for students to read three writing samples. You may wish to vary this slightly by reading the samples aloud as students listen. Either way, be sure students pause after each sample to complete the rating scale, showing how strong they believe the voice in each passage is. They should also come up with words to describe each voice. These words will help students create definitions later. You may wish to make class lists of words to describe each of the three voices.

Reflection

When students have had a chance to experience all three voices, they are invited to identify a favorite voice and a voice that sounds most like their own. Most students will likely choose Jack Gantos's voice as their favorite; it is probably the strongest of the three voices. If students do not think that any of the voices sound like their own, ask them to come up with a writer—anyone at all—whose voice is closest to theirs. Then ask them to look through their personal writing folders to find two words to describe their own voices.

In this reflection portion of the lesson, you may also wish to ask students to rank the three voices. Most should see Voice 3 as the strongest, Voice 1 as the next strongest, and Voice 2 as the weakest. The important question here, though, is *why*. When students know why they have ranked the samples as they did, they will be well on their way to constructing their personal definitions for voice.

Time to Define

Students will use what they have learned about voice to write a definition of it. Encourage students to look over their responses on pages 43 and 44 to write their definitions.

Share and Compare

In this part of the lesson, students have an opportunity to share their definitions of voice with classmates. You may also wish to share definitions with the class. Talk about what you hear, and compare it with your student rubric for voice. Did students come up with some voice features the rubric does not include?

Extending the Lesson

- Make a bulletin board display of students' definitions. You may also wish to add your own definition and those of some professional writers. Donald Murray, for instance, remarks that voice separates writing that is read from writing that is not read. Donald Graves compares voice in writing to the salt in stew—without it, there's no flavor!

- Take definitions to the next step, and create your own class checklist for strong voice. Post it where everyone can refer to it easily.

- Ask students to hunt for written passages (as short as one line, as long as one paragraph) that they think have strong voice. They should come to class prepared to read their choices aloud in their response groups.

- Is the power of voice in the writing or in the reading? Writers often debate this. Find out by having students read Voices 2 and 3 aloud. Can anyone read Voice 2 and make it sound energetic and exciting? Is it possible to read Voice 3 and make it sound dull? Why or why not? Discuss results with the class.

- Revise the weakest of the samples. (Most people agree that Voice 2 is the weakest, but Voice 1 may work as well.) Read results aloud to compare and talk about the strategies students used to strengthen the voice.

- Have each student look at a sample of his or her own writing, rate it on voice, and then revise it to bring the voice up at least one point. (Two points? Better yet!)

Voice and Expository Writing

For use with pages 46–49 in the Student Traitbook

In this lesson, students will review expository/ informational writing to learn how voice looks, sounds, and affects readers in this form.

Objectives

Students will recognize that although the voice of informational writing differs from that of narrative writing, voice still plays an important role in holding the attention of an audience. Students will deepen their understanding of voice by ranking samples and will sharpen their revision skills by enhancing the voice in a flat, voiceless passage.

Skills Focus

- Understanding that voice must change to match the form of writing
- Recognizing voice in informational writing
- Rating samples according to the amount of voice each projects
- Revising a flat piece of informational writing to make the voice stronger

Time Frame

Allow about 45 minutes for this lesson, excluding any extensions. The lesson can be divided into two parts if you wish. In part 1 (20 minutes), read and rank samples A, B, and C—again allowing time to debrief your results. Have each student discuss his or her rankings with a partner and with the class as a whole. In part 2 of the lesson (25 minutes), ask students to select one of the weaker samples and revise it for voice. Read results aloud.

Setting Up the Lesson

It's a surprise to many people, student writers included, that informational writing can be strong in voice. As a warm-up to this lesson, ask students to create a list of writing examples that are strong in voice. Now have them list examples that are weak in voice. Surprise them with examples of strong voice from informational sources. You may have a favorite source in mind; if not, use the Grade 6 *Daybook* listed in the Recommended Books for Teaching Voice, page 42 of this Teacher's Guide. It contains numerous read-aloud examples of strong informational writing. Other recommendations include the informational writings of Stephen J. Gould, Carl Sagan, Bill Nye the Science Guy, Bill Bryson, Thomas Cahill, Sneed B. Collard III, Faith Ringgold, Dorothy Hinshaw Patent, Michael L. Cooper, Julius Lester, David M. Schwartz, or any sample out of *Discover Magazine.* The example you choose can be short; the point is simply to show students that informational writing can be every bit as engaging as fiction—some people find it more so!

Teaching the Lesson

Read, Rate, and Rank

This portion of the lesson offers students a chance to assess voice by ranking samples of writing. You should feel free to read the samples aloud if you feel this will help your students. If possible, though, encourage them to read the samples on their own. Remind them to look and listen for strong voice as they read. This is an important skill for any writer to acquire. Writers must "hear" the voices of other writers in order to gain a sense of what voice is. Remind students to fill out the little chart at the end of each sample prior to making a final decision on the rankings.

Ranking by Voice

Students should work with a partner to review their voice charts from "Read, Rate, and Rank" and make a decision about which voice is strongest and which voice is weakest. When students have finished, have them share results with the class and discuss their responses to the three samples. Most students should see Sample A as the strongest. It is lively and directly written to the audience in a reader-friendly style. It includes interesting information and reflects the writer's knowledge of and enthusiasm for the topic. Sample C is the second strongest. The writer, who seems somewhat engaged with this topic, includes the interesting detail about the 9-inch statue. However, the writer misses several opportunities for strong voice by including generalizations about Senefru being a more benevolent leader than Khufu and the pyramid being built without slave labor. The passage that shows the weakest voice is definitely Sample B, which is encyclopedic in tone. The writer seems nearly asleep and is simply jotting down facts about Australia.

Discuss students' rankings and the reasons behind them. Ask students to defend their decisions by pointing to specific features or passages and identifying them as strong or weak in voice.

Revising for Voice

This is the students' chance to revise one of the weaker samples using what they have learned about strong voice. Encourage students to elaborate even if they invent some details. The purpose of this lesson is to build strong voice. Students should imagine that they are experts on Australia or on pyramids. They should write with confidence.

Extending the Lesson

- Read revisions aloud, and list techniques that student revisers used to strengthen the passages. Ask students to indicate which techniques they found especially effective.

- Have a weakest voice contest. Invite each student to write a short paragraph (five or six sentences) on a topic of his or her choice, making it as weak in voice as possible. Read the results aloud for fun; then ask students to explain what they did to keep the voice weak. Vote on the "winners."

- Have students revise one of the samples from the "weakest voice" contest. Read "before" and "after" results aloud.

- Have students give *you* a topic on which to write. Write a version with strong voice and a version with weak voice. Read both versions without telling students which version is which. Ask for their comments.

- Invite each student to look at a piece of his or her own writing and assess its voice. Then have students apply one technique you have discussed for strengthening voice, such as changing word choice, adding detail, adding humor, and using a more conversational tone.

"Hello, How Are You?" or "Waz Up?"

For use with pages 50–53 in the Student Traitbook

Writers develop distinctive and highly individual voices. For example, no one would mistake the voice of Jerry Seinfeld for that of Edgar Allan Poe. Even the most individual of voices can adapt to fit a particular purpose or audience. To do this, of course, the writer must know who his or her audience is and what sort of voice that audience is likely to respond to. In this lesson, students explore the importance of matching voice to audience.

Objectives

Students will learn to modify voice to fit the audience and to consider voice as an important factor in creating a piece of original writing.

Skills Focus

- Understanding the importance of audience in achieving the right voice
- Modifying a piece of writing to match the audience
- Creating original writing to match the needs of an identified audience

Time Frame

Allow about 60 minutes for this lesson, excluding extensions. You can divide the lesson into two parts. In part 1 (30 minutes), ask students to analyze the passage by Diane Stanley on page 51 of the Student Traitbook, paying particular attention to the voice Stanley projects through Mrs. Sump. Also have students complete the portion of the lesson under "A Different Voice," assuming the role of Mrs. Sump. In part 2 of the lesson (30 minutes), have students create side-by-side letters under "Writing for Two Different Audiences."

Setting Up the Lesson

List the types of writing your students have done recently, such as lists, letters, notes, diary or journal entries, personal reminders, assignments of various kinds, and so forth. Add to the list examples of the types of writing you have done. Now, identify the various audiences for which each piece was written, keeping in mind that sometimes a writer's audience is himself or herself. Finally, talk about how the voice of various pieces changed as the audiences changed. Does a report for a science class sound the same as a note to a friend? Does it sound the same as a personal entry in a diary? Why or why not?

Ask students to describe the different voices they have used in their own writing. Describe some of the voices you have used as well. Ideally, you will see some range, from very informal to quite formal. **Hint:** If your students do not have a sufficiently wide range of audiences to require different voices, feel free to add some hypothetical writing situations: Suppose you wrote a letter to the president? The manager of a local company? A relative you have never met? Your best friend who just moved away? A celebrity or author you admire?

Teaching the Lesson

Sharing an Example:
Saving Sweetness
Students can read to themselves the excerpt from Diane Stanley's *Saving Sweetness*. If they have difficulty with the dialect, however, you should be prepared to read it aloud to give them the true flavor of Mrs. Sump's folksy and somewhat insensitive voice. This is important because students need to describe the voice and then describe how the voice might shift slightly if Mrs. Sump were describing the same incident to a neighbor.

Reflecting
After students have had a chance to read the sample from *Saving Sweetness*, take a moment to talk about it. What did they think about the passage? What sort of person is Mrs. Sump? How can they tell? Give students time to complete the reflection activities, coming up with two words to describe Mrs. Sump's voice and two techniques Stanley uses to achieve this voice (dialect, Mrs. Sump's correcting herself [*escaped* to *disappeared, alive* to *safe*], informal language, Mrs. Sump's yelling). Have student pairs compare their responses, and ask them to share their reflections with the class.

A Different Voice
Have students use their imaginations to create the voice of Mrs. Sump speaking to a friend or neighbor. Would

she be meaner than when speaking to the sheriff? Would she be more honest about her feelings? What sort of language would she use? Feel free to ask these or other prompting questions to help set your students up for this writing activity.

Share and Compare

Give students time to share their new Mrs. Sump voices with partners. Invite a few volunteers to share their versions with the class. Share your version of Mrs. Sump, too! Also discuss the words students used to describe these different voices. Which student created the greatest difference between the first Mrs. Sump and the second? How did he or she do it?

Writing for Two Different Audiences

Creating a different voice for Mrs. Sump was a warm-up for this part of the lesson, in which students create two letters on the same topic—but for two different audiences. Each letter will tell about a school bully, but one letter will be to a friend and the other letter will be to a teacher or principal. (Students can come up with different audiences, but the two choices must prompt different voices.) Before students write, you may wish to discuss the expectations of each audience. Encourage student writers to put equal energy and detail into each piece.

Share and Compare

Ask student pairs to share with each other first, reminding them not to tell partners which letter is which. (Have them guess!) Then, invite volunteers to share letters with the class, asking listeners to match the correct letter with the intended audience. Share your own versions, too. Can students tell the difference?

Extending the Lesson

- Ask students to write a journal entry about Mrs. Sump in the voice of the sheriff or the little girl, Sweetness. What might the sheriff or Sweetness say? What voice would each use?

- Ask students to work in small groups and find two distinctive voices (two different voices per group) from current literature. They should be prepared to read these voices aloud to the class without disclosing the *source* of each. They can share the names of the writers but not tell which passage goes with which voice. Listeners should match the author to the voice and then say who the audience might be.

- Demonstrate advertisers' awareness of audience by collecting advertisements of various kinds. Read each advertisement aloud, and talk about who the audience most likely is.

From Flat to Fantastic

For use with pages 54–57 in the Student Traitbook

You know the old cliché: *I'm not sure what I'm looking for, but I'll know it when I see it.* **That old saying is true for most readers when it comes to voice. Even if a reader is not familiar with the concept of voice, he or she is almost certain to react emotionally to writing that is strong in voice. Voice helps the reader picture what a writer is describing and feel what that writer wants the reader to feel. This lesson is about helping students tune in to that power.**

Objectives

Students will use the strategies to revise writing that is weak in voice.

Skills Focus

- Looking more deeply at the trait of voice
- Comparing two passages, one strong in voice, the other weak in voice
- Identifying writing techniques or qualities that contribute to voice
- Connecting voice to imagery and feelings
- Revising a flat piece of writing to give it voice

Time Frame

Allow about 50 minutes for this lesson. You can divide the lesson into two parts. In part 1 (25 minutes), take students through "Seeing and Feeling," in which they'll comment on two writing samples. In part 2 (25 minutes), invite students to revise flat writing.

Setting Up the Lesson

This lesson focuses on what readers see and feel when they read writing that is strong in voice. Use the books recommended for this unit, which offer many examples for short read-alouds brimming with voice or choose a favorite passage of your own. As students listen to an example of strong voice, ask them to make brief notes on what they see or feel. Compare responses. Then, do the same with a sample that is weak in voice. If you cannot find an example you want, choose one of the weaker overhead sample writings for voice. (See Sample Papers 9–12 on pages 144–155.) Again, ask students to record what they see or feel. Compare the two examples—you should see a striking difference!

Teaching the Lesson

Sharing an Example: *Bull Run*

As students read this passage from Paul Fleischman's *Bull Run,* invite them to interact with the text, marking words or phrases that clearly show the writer's voice. Students can underline words or write in the margins. This will help them later when they must identify what Fleischman does to create voice. You may also wish to ask volunteers to read the passage aloud so that students can hear it more than once. Encourage volunteers to put plenty of feeling into the reading so that students can connect with poor Toby's plight.

Get the Voice Out

Ask a second volunteer to read the second sample aloud so that students can really hear differences between Fleischman's original and this poorly "revised" version. Again, invite students to mark up the text, especially noting places where voice seems weak or flat.

Seeing and Feeling

In this part of the lesson, students will focus more closely on the two passages, asking themselves, "Exactly what do I see? What do I feel?" for each one. They may look back at the passages and at their notes as they complete this portion.

Give students time to compare responses to the two passages with partners. Share a few thoughts with the class.

Where Is the Voice Coming From?

In a brief class discussion, try to identify specific techniques Fleischman uses to create stronger voice in his version. How does the first sample differ from the second? (Possible responses: Stronger language [*desperate, hotfooted*], a more vivid picture of the recruiter, dialogue, Toby's honesty about telling a "monstrous lie," and feeling "hot all over" because he's about to be embarrassed.)

**From Flat to Fantastic:
"Greenway Forest"**

Here is an opportunity for students to apply what they have learned about voice by revising a flat, uninteresting piece of writing that is weak in voice. Remind them to read through the passage thoroughly before beginning their revisions, underlining or noting sections that particularly need rewording. It is fine if students invent some details for their revisions. The point is to breathe some life into this tired piece.

As students share paragraphs with partners, groups, or the class, encourage listeners to notice specific differences between the original "Greenway Forest" and the revised version. What specific things did writers do to improve the text?

Extending the Lesson

- Make a list of strategies your writers used to improve voice in "Greenway Forest." How do their techniques compare with those used by professional writer Paul Fleischman in *Bull Run?*

- Choose a few more passages from Fleischman's classic book *Bull Run,* and invite student volunteers to read them aloud. With six to ten readers, you will create a kind of mini-drama about the Civil War and how various individuals responded to their experiences during the war. Then, invite students to comment on passages that were particularly effective.

- Create your own "voiceless challenges." Ask students to work in groups of three and identify a piece of writing that is strong in voice. Then, ask each group to rewrite that passage, taking out as much voice as possible. (They should think about what kinds of changes they are making as they do this.) Have groups exchange weak passages and then revise to put voice into the passage. Compare revisions to the authors' originals by reading aloud. Were your student authors able to come up with some of the same techniques professional writers use?

- Invite each student to find a piece of his or her own writing that needs improvement in voice. Students should read through the text, mark passages that need work, and revise, adding small details, stronger language, imagery, dialogue, or anything else that will bring the passage to life.

Voice

Teacher's Guide pages 41, 144–155
Transparency numbers 9–12

Objective

Students will review and apply what they have learned about the trait of voice.

Reviewing Voice

Review with students what they have learned about the trait of voice. Ask students to discuss what voice means and to explain why it is important in a piece of writing. Then ask them to recall the main points about voice that are discussed in Unit 3. Students' responses should include the following points:

- Understand the trait of voice.
- Use the appropriate voice for the task.
- Temper voice to match the needs of the audience.
- Revise to strengthen voice.

Applying Voice

To help students apply what they have learned about the trait of voice, distribute copies of the Student Rubric for Voice on page 41 of this Teacher's Guide. Students will use these to score one or more of the sample papers that begin on page 116. The papers for voice are also on overhead transparencies 9–12.

Before students score the papers, explain that a rubric is a grading system to determine the score a piece of writing should receive for a particular trait. Preview the Student Rubric for Voice, pointing out that a paper very strong in voice receives a score of 6 and a paper very weak in voice receives a score of 1. Tell students to read the rubric and then read the paper to be scored. Then tell them to look at the paper and rubric together to determine the score the paper should receive. Encourage students to make notes on each paper to help them score it. For example, they might put a check mark next to a sentence in which a strong voice emerges.

Overview

Throughout this unit, students will use sensory language to make readers part of the writer's experience, build vocabulary through the use of word graphics, revise writing to take it from flat to lively, and cut excess language to make writing concise and readable.

The focus of the instruction in this unit will be

- using sensory language to create a vivid picture
- using synonyms and antonyms to expand understanding of a word
- replacing flat, colorless language with specifics
- cutting clutter from wordy passages

Word Choice: *A Definition*

Word choice is the selection of appropriate words to fit audience, topic, and purpose. Good word choice should be clear, colorful and precise, and should help readers see, hear, and feel the world of the writer. The secrets to successful word choice include simplicity, use of powerful verbs, sensory detail, and, of course, variety—all of which come from an expanded vocabulary. In a business letter, writing must be brisk, clear, and to the point. A technical or research report calls for knowledge of content expressed through the skillful use of a specialized vocabulary. A poem or personal narrative allows the writer more freedom to use words in unexpected ways. Regardless of form, however, strong word choice leaves a reader saying, "I wish *I'd* written that!"

The Unit at a Glance

The following lessons in the Teacher's Guide and practice exercises in the Student Traitbook will help develop understanding of the trait of word choice. The Unit Summary provides an opportunity to practice evaluating papers for word choice.

Unit Overview: Word Choice

Teacher's Guide pages 56–60

The unique features of the trait of word choice are presented along with rubrics and a list of recommended literature for teaching word choice.

Lesson 13: Feeding Your Reader's Brain

Teacher's Guide pages 61–63
Student Traitbook pages 59–62

Sensory language enriches the reader's experience and helps make meaning clear by bringing the reader into the writer's world. In this lesson, students practice identifying and using sensory words and phrases.

Lesson 14: Word Graphics

Teacher's Guide pages 64–66
Student Traitbook pages 63–66

Knowledge of synonyms and antonyms can enrich a writer's understanding of language. In this lesson, students use word graphics to expand their knowledge of a key word.

Lesson 15: Specify to Clarify

Teacher's Guide pages 67–69
Student Traitbook pages 67–70

This lesson offers students practice in recognizing precise language, revising writing to make it sharper, and creating original text that is lively and explicit.

Lesson 16: Cut the Clutter!

Teacher's Guide pages 70–72
Student Traitbook pages 71–74

Some writers do not know when to stop writing. In this lesson, students practice recognizing wordy text and cutting clutter.

Unit Summary: Word Choice

Teacher's Guide page 73
Overhead numbers 13–16

Use the student rubric on page 59 and the activities in the Summary to practice assessing writing for the trait of word choice. Remember, 5-point rubrics, along with rationales for scores on sample papers, appear in the Appendix of this Teacher's Guide, pages 192–214.

Teacher Rubric for Word Choice

6
- The writing is clear, striking, original, and precise.
- The writer uses powerful verbs to give the writing energy.
- Sensory language, as appropriate, greatly enhances meaning.
- The writing is concise; each word counts.

5
- The writing is clear and often original. Words are generally used accurately.
- The writer relies more on strong verbs than on modifiers to enrich meaning.
- Sensory language, as appropriate, adds important detail or enhances mood.
- The writing is reasonably concise; a word or phrase here and there could be cut.

4
- The writing is clear in most cases. A few words or phrases are vague, confusing, or inaccurate.
- The writer uses some strong verbs—and may or may not rely too heavily on modifiers.
- Sensory language is present, if needed.
- Some writing is concise; wordy moments may crop up also.

3
- The writing is often unclear, misleading, or vague, though the main idea still comes through.
- The reader needs to hunt for strong verbs. Modifiers may be overused.
- Sensory language is either minimal or overused.
- The writing may be short but is not necessarily concise. Some clutter is evident.

2
- Many words and phrases are misused, vague, or unclear. The reader must guess at the writer's main message.
- Strong verbs are rare.
- Sensory language is minimal or absent.
- Word use may be skeletal or cluttered; either way, meaning is hard to determine.

1
- Words and phrases are consistently vague, confusing, or misused.
- Verbs are weak throughout; the writing lacks energy.
- Sensory language is missing.
- Word choice seems random. Words create no clear meaning.

Student Rubric for Word Choice

6
- Every word contributes to the main message.
- My verbs are powerful and give the writing energy and life.
- Sensory words and phrases paint a clear, vivid picture in the reader's mind.
- I got rid of any clutter. Every word counts.

5
- Most of my words and phrases are clear.
- I used a lot of strong verbs.
- I used sensory words to help paint pictures in the reader's mind.
- I got rid of most clutter. I don't think it's a problem.

4
- My words are usually clear. The reader can figure out my main idea.
- I used some strong verbs. I guess I could use more.
- Some of my words paint pictures. Some are vague or general.
- My writing has some clutter. I could cut some words or phrases.

3
- My word choice is unclear in many places. The reader might guess my main idea.
- I think I have some verbs. I am sure I need more.
- The reader might be able to picture what I am talking about if he or she works at it.
- My writing is cluttered. I used too many words I did not need, or else my descriptions are too sketchy.

2
- My words are very unclear. I did not always know the meaning myself.
- I do not know for sure whether I used verbs. I am not sure what a verb is.
- When I read this aloud, I think it's hard to picture what I am talking about.
- I do not know for sure whether I used too many words or not enough words. I just wrote.

1
- My words are hard to understand. They are vague—or I just guessed which word to use.
- I do not know whether I used verbs. What is a verb?
- When I read this aloud, a lot of the words do not make sense to me.
- Maybe I used too many words. Maybe I used the wrong words. I don't know.

Recommended Books for Teaching Word Choice

As you share literature, draw attention to the word choice. Ask students questions like these: *Can you tell the meaning of new words from context? Does the writer use words in a fresh, original way? Do you hear any strong verbs? Does this writing seem wordy, sketchy, or about right?*

Burleigh, Robert. 1997. *Hoops.* New York: Harcourt Brace and Company. Take-your-breath-away power in language that captures the rhythm of a basketball game.

Claggett, Fran, Louann Reid, and Ruth Vinz. 1999. *Daybook of Critical Reading and Writing, Grade 6.* Wilmington, MA: Great Source Education Group, Inc. Outstanding excerpts from the best of modern literature combine with challenging writing tasks that touch on many word choice–related skills and concepts.

Collard, Sneed B. III. 2000. *Acting for Nature: What Young People Around the World Are Doing to Protect the Environment.* Berkeley, CA: Heyday Books. Good, clear use of language in nonfiction writing; effective use of scientific terminology in context.

Cooper, Michael L. 1999. *Indian School: Teaching the White Man's Way.* New York: Clarion Books. Particularly crisp, clear, concise language in nonfiction.

Lowry, Lois. 1980. *Autumn Street.* New York: Houghton Mifflin. Outstanding examples of words used effectively to create imagery.

Myers, Walter Dean. 2001. *Bad Boy: A Memoir.* New York: HarperCollins. Strong sensory details bring Harlem to life in the memoir of this great author.

Paulsen, Gary. 2000. *Hatchet.* New York: Simon & Schuster. Many students will be familiar with this book. Look again at selected passages, appreciating Paulsen's gift for verbs and powerful images—sensory language abounds.

Sebranek, Patrick, Dave Kemper, and Verne Meyer. 1999. *Write Source 2000.* Wilmington, MA: Great Source Education Group, Inc. Information on verbs, sensory details, context clues, modifiers, use of the dictionary, figurative language, and idioms.

Snicket, Lemony. 2001. *The Hostile Hospital* (A Series of Unfortunate Events, Book 8). New York: HarperCollins. Snicket's playful style is reminiscent of Roald Dahl's. Use it to illustrate strong verbs and Snicket's specialty: deriving meaning from context and introducing new words. This book is excellent for teaching voice.

Warren, Andrea. 2001. *We Rode the Orphan Trains.* Boston: Houghton Mifflin Company. Clear, concise, and simple language brings nonfiction to life.

Feeding Your Reader's Brain

For use with pages 58–62 in the Student Traitbook

Sensory language does more than make meaning clear. It brings the reader into the writer's world with details of sight, sound, smell, taste, and touch. This lesson heightens students' awareness of the power of such language and invites them to use sensory words and phrases, as appropriate, to make writing clear and appealing.

Objectives

Students will identify sensory language in the writing of others and then use the listing of sensory details as a prewriting strategy in creating a descriptive paragraph.

Skills Focus

- Understanding the concept of sensory language
- Identifying sensory details in a passage from literature
- Organizing sensory details within a chart
- Listing sensory details as a prewriting activity
- Creating original text rich with sensory detail

Time Frame

Allow about 45 minutes for this lesson. The lesson can be divided into two parts. In part 1 (20 minutes), students should review the passage from *Town Early*, identify sensory details, and then create a sensory detail chart based on the passage called "The Tornado." In part 2 (25 minutes), students should build on what they have learned by creating a sensory detail list (under "Your Turn to Write") then using that list to write an original descriptive paragraph based on an outdoor experience.

Setting Up the Lesson

Use page 58 to introduce (or review) the trait of word choice. Point out the bulleted items, which tell students what they will be working on.

It is important for students to know what sensory language is and to understand its power in creating a vivid impression for the reader. Ask students to imagine themselves in a place that appeals to all senses. Good possibilities might include a circus, a restaurant, a carnival—or the beach or a forest. Start with a flat description, such as *It was interesting at the beach!* or *The circus was a busy place!* What do your students picture from this description? Probably not much! Now, tell students that together you are going to create a picture that appeals to all senses— sight, hearing, smell, taste, and touch. Brainstorm details from each category. You do not need to create the piece of writing that would go with these details—though you could. Students will get the idea!

Teaching the Lesson

Sharing an Example: *Town Early*
Students can read to themselves this short excerpt from *Town Early*—or you can read it aloud if you prefer. Ask students to simply listen and/or look for sensory details during the first reading. Remind them that sensory details include what they can see, hear, smell, taste, and touch. They may not find examples from *every* category, (for instance, there are no taste details), but they should find many sensory words and phrases in this passage.

Sensory Reaction
Students should read through the *Town Early* example again, this time underlining sensory details. They should work with partners to do this, and then they should check their findings against the list in the chart. Note: Most students should find more details than the few that are listed here. Be sure to commend students for finding details not included in the chart.

Creating Your Own Chart
Students should build on what they have learned by creating a second chart based on the passage "The Tornado." Like *Town Early,* this passage is filled with sensory details. This time, students should work on their own, but they can share findings with a partner and with the class. At this point, everyone should have a clear

understanding of the concept of sensory detail. Also discuss the impact of sensory details on the reader.

Your Turn to Write

In the last major segment of the lesson, students brainstorm a list of personal details that form the basis of a descriptive paragraph. They should complete the list quickly, jotting down whatever comes to mind. Instead of trying to fill out every category, students should focus on what is clear and vivid. In writing their paragraphs, students should select the *best* sensory details they have identified rather than trying to use every one (which would result in wordy, overwritten text). Allow time for students to share writings within small groups and with the class as a whole.

Extending the Lesson

- Make a poster that lists the advantages of using sensory language in writing. Encourage students to think from the reader's point of view.

- Invite students to hunt for writing that includes good sensory details. (Advertisements, expository science writing, and travel brochures are good sources.) Ask students to read passages aloud while others listen for the sensory details that "speak" to them.

- What literature are students currently reading in class? Is it strong or weak in sensory detail? Ask students to search for passages that illustrate strong sensory detail or the lack of it.

- Invite students to create two pieces of writing based on the same topic: one rich in sensory details, one weak in sensory details. Have students read passages aloud and compare them.

- Challenge students, in groups, to create passages without sensory details for other groups to revise. The difficulty here lies in omitting all sensory details from the challenge paragraph. Ask students to exchange challenge paragraphs and revise them—then they may read the results aloud.

Word Graphics

For use with pages 63–66 in the Student Traitbook

In this lesson, students use word graphics displaying synonyms and antonyms to more deeply explore the meaning of a word.

Objectives

Students will understand what synonyms and antonyms are and will create word graphics to build knowledge of a key word.

Skills Focus

- Understanding what synonyms and antonyms are
- Knowing how to find synonyms and antonyms for a given word
- Using word graphics to display synonyms and antonyms
- Using knowledge of synonyms and antonyms to deepen understanding of word meaning
- Expanding vocabulary by making word graphics part of a personal dictionary

Time Frame

Allow about 30 minutes for this lesson.

Setting Up the Lesson

Make sure students have access to a dictionary and a thesaurus. Explain that they will probably need to refer to one or both books in the course of this lesson. Ask students whether they know what a synonym is and discuss their responses, making sure that everyone understands. Provide examples on the overhead or board. Do the same with antonyms, listing several examples orally and in writing to ensure that everyone gets the idea. Let students know that they will be building two kinds of graphics: lists (or ladders) for synonyms and sequences for antonyms. Model these so that students can envision them. Also emphasize that the purpose of the lesson is to deepen understanding of a word by exploring synonyms and antonyms for that word.

Teaching the Lesson

Sharing an Example:
Grandmother's Pigeon

Students can read the excerpt from *Grandmother's Pigeon* on their own. As they read, they should look for two or three words they find especially interesting. Each should be a word the student wishes to explore further. Students should share word lists with partners, discussing which words they found most interesting and why.

The First Step: What *Kind* of Word Is It?

It is difficult to suggest synonyms and antonyms without knowing what part of speech a particular word is. A noun must have another noun as a synonym: *grouch* and *curmudgeon* are synonyms, for example, while *grouch* and *cheerful* are not. Briefly review the definitions of nouns, verbs, adjectives, and adverbs. Also make sure that students know how to locate a word's part of speech in the dictionary.

Building a Synonym Ladder

This portion of the lesson asks students to suggest two synonyms for the word *fragile.* They can use a dictionary or thesaurus to help them locate synonyms. Share some examples aloud, and encourage students to add words to their personal dictionaries *throughout* the lesson.

An Antonym Sequence

Remind students that the graphic for this portion of the lesson will look different because it is meant to show contrast. Antonyms are opposites. Also remind students that just as a word can have more than one synonym, it can have more than one antonym. Illustrate this using a simple word everyone knows, such as *good.* Antonyms might be *bad, evil, wicked, malicious,* and so on. Or, depending on how the word is used (for example, if it refers to food), antonyms might include *tasteless, disgusting, flavorless,* and so forth.

Students will complete a simple warm-up, using the word *tiny*. They need to find only one antonym and one "middle word," a word whose definition falls somewhere between the key word and its antonym. Then, they are ready for the more complex graphics contained in the second part of the lesson. These graphics include both synonyms and antonyms.

Extending the Lesson

- Ask some or all of your students to do oral presentations of two to three minutes, using the graphics to explain the word to the class. A good way to do this is to have teams ask class members (prior to sharing the graphic) to quickly jot down one synonym and one antonym for the key word. Then, they can share their graphics and compare.

- Challenge students to give you key words for which you will find synonyms, antonyms, or both. Do what you can on the spot; then, if you need more time, look in a dictionary or a thesaurus, and create a graphic on the overhead or board.

- Have a synonym or antonym contest. The rules are simple. One team of two students comes up with a very simple word that everyone knows. Then, everyone gets two minutes to see how many synonyms or antonyms he or she can come up with. The person with the longest list of legitimate synonyms and antonyms wins a prize (an extra day to complete an assignment, reduced homework, extra points, and so on).

Lesson 15

Specify to clarify

For use with pages 67–70 in the Student Traitbook

Advertisers know the value of precise language. No serious advertiser tells the public, "Boy, this is a good car here! You'll like it!" They make sure listeners know that their vehicle is the best, with "cornering capabilities a jackrabbit could only hope for, leather seats to rival your best couch, a sound system that makes you feel you're at a concert, and enough power to keep you in the fast lane." Precise language decreases the odds that a reader will misinterpret the writer's message. This lesson is all about making writing more vivid and precise.

Objectives

Students will learn to recognize vivid language, revise flat writing to make it more precise, and use clear, lively language in their writing.

Skills Focus

- Identifying examples of lively, specific word choice
- Revising flat writing to improve the word choice
- Creating original writing in which the word choice is precise and vivid

Time Frame

Allow about 40 minutes for this lesson, excluding any extensions.

Setting Up the Lesson

Advertisements and menus offer excellent examples of colorful, precise language. Advertisement writers know that if the language is flat or vague, consumers are less likely to purchase the products. Take advantage of these specialized writers' skills by using their work to illustrate how important vivid word choice can be. Find some examples to share with your students. Then create your own flat versions for contrast.

> *"The difference between the right word and the almost-right word is the difference between lightning and a lightning-bug."*
>
> —Mark Twain

Teaching the Lesson

Sharing an Example: Lives of the Artists

Students can read the excerpt from Kathleen Krull's *Lives of the Artists* to themselves, underlining examples of clear, vivid writing as they go. Encourage them to read through the passage more than once—it's easy to miss details!

Share and Compare

Students should share with partners, discuss words or phrases they've selected, and complete the short list on page 68 of the Student Traitbook.

A Short Warm-Up

This warm-up calls for students to do some brief revising and writing. The idea is to delete vague language that tells the reader almost nothing and replace it with stronger word choices that make the meaning clear and paint vivid pictures in the reader's mind. An example is provided.

Share and Compare

After completing the three unrevised sentences, each student should share results with a partner by reading aloud and comparing revision techniques. Encourage volunteers to share their revisions with the class as well.

Putting the Reader at the Scene

You may wish to encourage a brief prewriting activity for this portion of the lesson, in which students are asked to create vivid descriptions of their own. It may help to list details or create a word web for the person being described. Encourage students to think of unusual details and words that will capture the individual's personality or character. HINT: Specific things a person has said or done tell much more than generalizations. We know that Leonardo unleashed a lizard at one party. What does that tell us about him?

Share and Compare

Give students time to share their descriptions with partners or in small groups. Encourage listeners to jot down words or phrases that catch their attention. Listeners can also ask questions. After sharing, students should feel free to change, delete, or add words and phrases to improve the writing further.

Extending the Lesson

- In the spirit of good revision, ask students to put their descriptive writing away for a few days and then return to it. This will help them see their work with fresh eyes. Then have them revise again for word choice. Give them time to work on the pieces a bit more. Discuss any revisions students have made.

- Invite students to look for samples of colorful or precise language in any literature they are currently reading. Samples could come from poems, novels, nonfiction writing, textbooks, magazines, and newspapers. Gather as many as possible and read them aloud.

- Ask students to create a piece of tired writing for you to revise. It should be no more than four sentences long and as colorless as they can make it. With students' help, revise it on the overhead transparency. Be sure to share "before" and "after" samples with students.

- Continue the one-sentence "before and after" practice routinely with students. You can put a flat sentence on the overhead, ask everyone to revise it, and then read the results. Or have students write their own "before" sentences and exchange them with partners. Creating lessons is wonderful practice for beginning writers!

Lesson 16

Cut the clutter!

For use with pages 71–74 in the Student Traitbook

In an effort to come up with the right word or words, some writers use a bushel of words when a teaspoon would do nicely. This lesson shows students how to avoid wordy, boring writing by learning to spot—and cut—the clutter.

Objectives

Students will identify clutter in two samples of wordy writing and practice revision skills to revise and improve each sample.

Skills Focus

- Understanding that wordy writing is also ineffective writing
- Identifying wordiness (clutter) in a sample of writing
- Revising to reduce or eliminate clutter

Time Frame

Allow about 50 minutes for this lesson, excluding any extensions. You can divide the lesson into two parts, providing revision practice in each. In part 1 (25 minutes), work on the airplane example, pages 71–72 of the Student Traitbook, through the "Share and Compare" portion of the lesson, page 73. In part 2 (25 minutes), begin with "Cleaning Out the Clutter," page 73, giving students time to revise the rainy day example and to share results.

Setting Up the Lesson

Wordy writing is ineffective because it causes readers to lose focus. You can readily illustrate this by asking students whether they know of anyone who talks too much and never seems to stop! Discuss reactions to this, and then read the following example to illustrate what wordiness sounds like (exaggerate—ham it up!): *Today class, we'll be working on wordiness and I'm delighted to be working on this problem which is such a problem for many writers because wordiness gets in the way of good writing and if we can eliminate wordiness, we can improve a lot of writing, so let's begin!*

> *"Short words are best and the old words are best of all."*
>
> —Winston Churchill

Teaching the Lesson

Sharing an Example

Students will revise the piece on pages 71–72 of the Student Traitbook about being on an airplane. Students should read the passage before beginning any revision and then complete the survey under "My Thoughts." Most students will agree that the passage is very wordy, but you should certainly discuss this if some students disagree. Following the discussion, students should work with partners to eliminate any unnecessary language. Remind students that cutting can leave ragged edges. They should feel free to "patch" their revisions by changing punctuation or by adding transitional words where appropriate.

Let's Compare

Here, students have a chance to compare their revisions of the airplane piece with the suggested version. If students' revised versions show few cuts, encourage them to go back and read the example again. Could more cuts be made without sacrificing meaning? Have students cut as much as possible without hurting the message.

Share and Compare

Make sure that students complete the self-evaluation under Share and Compare, page 73. Allow time for student pairs to discuss their evaluations.

Cleaning Out the Clutter

As revisers, students should ask themselves, "Do I need to be more ruthless when I revise for wordiness?" Have students use what they learned from revising the airplane piece to help them revise the rainy day paragraph on page 73 of the Student Traitbook. You may wish to display an overhead copy of this paragraph to show your version after students are finished. (Do not let them see you work while they are still cutting!) Here is the suggested result, which you may wish to read aloud:

When I woke up, I looked out the big front window to see that it was raining for the thirty-fifth day in a row. It's a record for our part of the country, so the news stations would be talking about it all day. This is nothing to celebrate. It's winter! The news *should* be about why it hasn't snowed.

Extending the Lesson

- Share with the class results from students' revisions. Did those who cut the most leave out anything important? In cutting a wordy piece down to size, is it all right to eliminate *some* details? How can students tell?

- Post some of the shorter revisions, along with the original text. It helps many students to *see*—as well as hear—results of this kind of revision.

- Invite students to revise pieces of their own writing to weed out wordiness. Remind students that *all* writers do this. It does not mean that the original writing was poorly done. Revising writing is part of the writing process, and it usually means finding a more concise way to express thoughts.

- Tell students to be on the lookout for wordy writing wherever it may hide! Make a bulletin board display of wondrous wordiness, and offer extra credit to students who cut wordy pieces down to size.

Word Choice

Teacher's Guide pages 59, 156–167
Transparency numbers 13–16

Objective

Students will review and apply what they have learned about the trait of word choice.

Reviewing Word Choice

Review with students what they have learned about the trait of word choice. Ask students to discuss what word choice means and to explain why it is important in a piece of writing. Then ask them to recall the main points about word choice that are discussed in Unit 4. Students' responses should include the following points:

- Use sensory language to create vivid pictures.
- Expand word meanings with synonyms and antonyms.
- Use specific words.
- Cut out unnecessary words.

Applying Word Choice

To help students apply what they have learned about the trait of word choice, distribute copies of the Student Rubric for Word Choice on page 59 of this Teacher's Guide. Students will use these to score one or more of the sample papers that begin on page 116. The papers for word choice are also on overhead transparencies 13–16.

Before students score the papers, explain that a rubric is a grading system to determine the score a piece of writing should receive for a particular trait. Preview the Student Rubric for Word Choice, pointing out that a paper very strong in word choice receives a score of 6 and a paper very weak in word choice receives a score of 1. Tell students to read the rubric and then read the paper to be scored. Then tell them to look at the paper and rubric together to determine the score the paper should receive. Encourage students to make notes on each paper to help them score it. For example, they might underline strong verbs or descriptive language.

Unit 5

Sentence Fluency

Overview

The point of this unit is to help students see, hear, and think like readers as they create text that's readable. Writers who look and listen for the flow in a piece of writing usually come up with something smooth and pleasurable to read silently or aloud.

The focus of the instruction in this unit will be

- varying sentence length to create interest.
- eliminating awkward run-on sentences.
- revising text to make it fluent.
- exploring various components that contribute to fluency.

Sentence Fluency: *A Definition*

Sentence fluency is the rhythm and flow of language. It is more than how words look on the page; it is also how they play to the ear. Reading aloud is a good way to test fluency, since fluent writing invites strong, expressive reading. Sentences that vary in both structure and length contribute significantly to fluency by snapping the reader to attention— much the way a shift in musical rhythm helps wake up a sleepy listener. In general, a strong writer avoids repetition or run-ons, though either may be used sparingly by a skilled writer for stylistic effect. The fluent writer also recognizes the difference between complete sentences and fragments but may slip in a fragment to lend punch to the writing now and then. Though not a focus of this unit, good dialogue is also a component of fluency.

The Unit at a Glance

The following lessons in the Teacher's Guide and practice exercises in the Student Traitbook will help develop understanding of the trait of sentence fluency. The Unit Summary provides an opportunity to practice evaluating papers for sentence fluency.

Unit Overview: Sentence Fluency

Teacher's Guide pages 74–78   Students are introduced to the unique features of the trait of sentence fluency.

Lesson 17: Short, Long, and In-between

Teacher's Guide pages 79–81
Student Traitbook pages 75–79   Variety in sentence length is a vital component of fluent writing. In this lesson, students take a close-up look at sentence length, learn to assess writing for variety, and practice transforming monotonous prose into something more fluent.

Lesson 18: Catching Up to Run-on Sentences

Teacher's Guide pages 82–84
Student Traitbook pages 80–83   In this lesson, students learn to identify and revise two kinds of run-on sentences: Type A, two independent clauses joined without punctuation or connecting words, and Type B, the string of endless clauses and phrases joined by connecting words.

Lesson 19: From First to Last in Fluency

Teacher's Guide pages 85–87
Student Traitbook pages 84–87   Nonfluent writing has trouble hiding when text is read aloud. In this lesson, students use eyes and ears to rank three pieces for fluency. Then, they revise a weak piece to improve the fluency through any strategies they find appropriate.

Lesson 20: What Makes It Flow?

Teacher's Guide pages 88–90
Student Traitbook pages 88–91   A guided analysis helps students identify specific characteristics that can contribute to fluency in any piece of writing.

Unit Summary: Sentence Fluency

Teacher's Guide page 91
Overhead numbers 9–12   Use the student rubric on page 77 and the activities in the Summary to practice assessing writing for the trait of sentence fluency.

Teacher Rubric for Sentence Fluency

6
- The writing is smooth, natural, and easy to read.
- Variety in sentence length and structure is striking.
- The piece invites expressive oral reading that brings out the voice.
- The writer avoids run-ons and repetition.
- Dialogue, if used, sounds natural and conversational.

5
- The writing is smooth and quite easy to read.
- Variety in sentence length is noticeable.
- The piece is a pleasure to read aloud.
- Run-ons in the text are rare, if existent at all.
- Dialogue, if used, sounds natural.

4
- The writing is not difficult to read, despite an awkward moment or two.
- Some sentences begin differently; there is some variety in sentence length.
- It is easy to read this piece aloud with some rehearsal.
- Run-ons may appear but do not seriously impair fluency.
- Dialogue, if used, sounds reasonably natural, though a little forced in spots.

3
- The writing is sometimes easy to read. Choppy sentences or other problems may necessitate re-reading.
- Sentence beginnings tend to be alike; sentences tend to be similar in length.
- Rehearsal is definitely needed before reading this piece aloud.
- Run-ons may be a problem.
- Dialogue, if used, does not quite echo the way people actually speak.

2
- Choppy sentences, run-ons, or other problems slow the reader down.
- The writer uses little or no sentence variety to add interest to the text.
- This piece is hard to read aloud, even with rehearsal.
- Run-ons are likely to be a problem.
- Dialogue, if used, does not sound natural or conversational.

1
- The writing is consistently difficult to follow or read aloud.
- Sentence length shows little or no variation.
- The piece is very difficult to read aloud, even with rehearsal.
- Run-ons impair fluency.
- Dialogue, if used, is hard to follow or to separate from other text.

Student Rubric for Sentence Fluency

6
- My writing is clear, smooth, and easy to read. It flows!
- Sentences begin in many different ways. They range from short and snappy to long and smooth.
- It's easy to read this paper aloud with lots of expression.
- I avoided run-ons that could make my ideas hard to follow.
- If I used dialogue, it sounds like real people talking.

5
- My writing is clear and smooth most of the time. It's fairly easy to read.
- I notice a lot of variety in both length and structure.
- The variety makes it easy to read with some expression.
- I avoided run-ons. I think I caught them all.
- If I used dialogue, I did a good job. It sounds real to me.

4
- Some of my writing is smooth. Some is choppy or repetitive.
- There is some variety in length and structure—some repetition too, though!
- The reader can make this writing sound expressive if he or she works at it!
- I may have one or two run-ons, but I don't think they hurt the overall flow.
- My dialogue (if I used any) sounds fairly natural; it could use a little work.

3
- Short, choppy sentences or repetition slows the reader down.
- Many sentences begin the same way. Many are the same length.
- It is not easy to read this paper aloud, but you can do it.
- In reading again, I notice some run-ons—or else my writing is too choppy.
- If I used dialogue, I think I need to make it sound more natural.

2
- This writing is bumpy, full of choppy sentences, run-ons, and repetition.
- Too many sentences begin the same way. Too many are the same length.
- It is hard to read this aloud. I tried and it was hard even for me!
- Run-ons abound. It's hard to tell where sentences begin and end.
- I do not think my dialogue sounds like real people talking.

1
- I can't tell one sentence from another. Are these sentences?
- I'm not sure whether the beginnings are different. I'm not sure how long my sentences are!
- This is very hard to read aloud. I don't even want to try it myself.
- I'm pretty sure I used run-on sentences, but it is so hard to tell!
- Did I use dialogue? I'm not sure. It's hard to pick out the dialogue!

Recommended Books
for Teaching Sentence Fluency

Remember to ask students questions like these: *Do you hear variety in sentence length? What about beginnings or sentence patterns in general? Do you hear any run-ons? Does the dialogue sound natural?*

Allen, Thomas B. 2001. *Remember Pearl Harbor: American and Japanese Survivors Tell Their Stories.* Washington, D.C.: National Geographic Society. Gritty account of the Pearl Harbor attack told through voices from both sides of the battle.

Bridges, Ruby. 1999. *Through My Eyes.* New York: Scholastic. Stunning nonfiction account of the young girl who shook America to the core and inspired a generation to shun segregation in public schools.

Burleigh, Robert. 1997. *Hoops.* New York: Harcourt Brace & Company. Take-your-breath-away power in language that captures the rhythm and flow of a basketball game. Highly original. Fun to read aloud or to have students read and act out.

Claggett, Fran, Louann Reid, and Ruth Vinz. 1999. *Daybook of Critical Reading and Writing, Grade 6.* Wilmington, MA: Great Source Education Group, Inc. Outstanding excerpts from the best of modern literature combine with challenging writing tasks that touch on numerous sentence fluency-related skills and concepts.

Hesse, Karen. 2000. *Stowaway.* New York: Margaret K. McElderberry Books. Historical fiction written as a journal. Spare, poignant style students may enjoy imitating.

Hite, Sid. 2001. *Stick & Whittle.* New York: Scholastic. Rollicking adventure and story of friendship set in the Old West. Filled with fluent passages.

Ibbotson, Eva. 2002. *Journey to the River Sea.* New York: Penguin Putnam books for Young Readers. A sophisticated, wonderfully readable style. Strong dialogue.

Sebranek, Patrick, Dave Kemper and Verne Meyer. 1999. *Write Source 2000.* Wilmington, MA: Great Source Education Group, Inc. User-friendly information to sentence fluency-related concepts and strategies.

More Ideas

Looking for more ideas on using literature to teach the trait of sentence fluency? We recommend *Books, Lessons, Ideas for Teaching the Six Traits: Writing at Middle and High School,* published by Great Source. Compiled and annotated by Vicki Spandel. For information, please phone 800-289-4490.

Short, Long, and In-between

For use with pages 76–79 in the Student Traitbook

Monotony can be hard to take. Virtually everyone appreciates variety—in food, scenery, experiences, and writing. Variety in sentence length greatly enhances sentence fluency, and it's not that hard to achieve. Simply helping students notice sentence length is a good beginning. Next step: revising to break the monotony!

Objectives

Students will heighten their awareness of sentence variety by analyzing text and reading it aloud. They will then revise a passage that has almost no variety in order to make it more fluent.

Skills Focus

- Listening for variety as text is read aloud
- Analyzing the extent of variety in sentence length
- Revising to increase fluency by varying sentence length

Time Frame

Allow about 50 minutes for this lesson. The lesson can be divided into two parts, if you wish. In part 1 (30 minutes), students should review the passage from *Notes From A Liar and Her Dog,* by Gennifer Choldenko, and respond to the level of fluency. They should also read and discuss the short example under "My Turn" and count the number of words in each sentence. In part 2 (20 minutes), students should revise, share, and discuss the passage under "My Turn."

Setting Up the Lesson

The point of the lesson is that variety is critical to achieving fluency in writing. To show how monotonous lack of variety can be, you might begin with an example outside of school: say, food. What if students had to eat exactly the same thing (get them to name an item they find less than appealing) for every single meal for one week. How many could do it? How many would complain or stop eating altogether at some point?

Monotony is just as deadly in the world of writing. To prove the point, rewrite a small portion of the passage from the students' Introduction to this lesson, page 75 of the Student Traitbook (You won't need to read the whole passage). Ask them to look at the original in the Traitbook as you share your "revised" version. It might sound something like this: *Fluent writing is rhythmic and easy on the ear. Fluent writing is like a good piece of music. A song with jarring rhythm or lyrics is unpleasant. A song that is monotonous is unpleasant.*

Ask students how much they would enjoy reading if everything from newspapers to novels were written in this boring, monotonous way. (How many would complain? How many would avoid reading whenever possible?) Well then, time for a lesson in stomping out monotony.

Teaching the Lesson

Sharing an Example: *Notes From a Liar and Her Dog*

Students can read this short excerpt to themselves, or you can share it aloud one time through if you think that will help them hear the fluency. They should read the passage twice, once to get the main idea, and a second time to focus on sentence length, paying particular attention to variety. They do not need to count words; they should just get a general sense of how much variety is present (quite a lot).

Your Response

In this part of the lesson, students should first respond to the fluency (How much variety do they hear/see in Choldenko's passage?) and then check with a partner and discuss results. Most should hear a great deal of variety in this very fluent text.

Seeing the Numbers

The point here is not to suggest that students should count words each time they read. Rather, they should verify with numbers what their ears tell them: the passage has a lot of variety. Notice that the number of words in each sentence ranges from 3 to 29; that's more variety by far than most writers achieve. Ask students whether this number surprises them. Also ask how they rated the passage. If they did not hear much variety, why was that? (It's there!)

Your Turn to Crunch the Numbers

Students should read aloud the short passage under "Your Turn" to get a general impression of the fluency. You can take time to talk about this prior to their counting words in sentences. After discussing general impressions, ask students to do a count and to fill out the chart under "Your Turn to Crunch the Numbers." Do their numbers match their impressions? They should have heard very little variety, and the actual numbers will bear this out (5, 6, 6, 6, 5, 6, 6, 4, 5, 7, 6, 7, 6, 6, 6). Students should compare impressions with a partner and read the numbers aloud to emphasize the monotony. Close this section of the lesson by brainstorming a list of ways to eliminate sentence monotony, such as adding detail, combining sentences, eliminating unneeded sentences, changing sentence beginnings.

Revising for Variety

Using the list of strategies you brainstormed together during the previous section of the lesson, students should revise the monotonous passage on rain and snow. Encourage students to mark up the text first and then revise. They can make any changes they wish so long as the main idea of the passage remains intact. Encourage students to read revisions aloud to themselves first before sharing with a partner. Sometimes once through is not enough. They may need to make additional changes before the passage seems sufficiently fluent. Only reading aloud will let them know when the revision is done!

Remind students to listen for fluency—not just look at text. They need to hear it aloud. Suggest that they not look at the text as it is being read, but simply listen. What improvements do they hear? Share some samples with the class.

Extending the Lesson

- Do your own revision of the rain/snow paragraph on an overhead. Do not show it to students until they have finished their revisions. Then let them see and hear yours. How did you do? Were your changes significant, or did you revise with a light touch?

- Invite students to do a sentence-by-sentence word-count analysis of any piece of original writing from their own writing folders. What does this analysis tell them about the amount of variety in their writing? Provide time for any revision that they think is necessary.

- Make a poster based on the ideas you brainstormed for eliminating monotony in sentence length. Post it in class for student reference.

Lesson 18

Catching Up to Run-on Sentences

For use with pages 80–83 in the Student Traitbook

Run-ons get in the way of fluency primarily because they make reading difficult; the reader often cannot tell where to stop or start—and may run out of breath if the writer goes on too long! In this lesson, students learn to identify and revise run-ons to improve fluency.

Objectives

Students will learn to recognize two different types of run-on sentences and will apply specific strategies for eliminating run-ons in their own writing or the writing of others.

Skills Focus

- Understanding how run-ons affect fluency
- Recognizing run-ons in which two independent clauses are run together without punctuation or connecting words
- Recognizing run-ons in which endless connecting words join a string of clauses or phrases
- Revising someone else's text to eliminate run-on problems
- Revising personal text to eliminate run-ons

Time Frame

Allow about 50 minutes for this lesson, excluding any extensions.

Setting Up the Lesson

It is critical to this lesson that students understand what a run-on sentence is and recognize its effect on sentence fluency. Examples are very helpful. On the overhead or on the board, write three separate examples, one with sound sentence structure, one representing a Type A run-on problem, and one representing a type B run-on problem. (Type A—two independent clauses joined without punctuation or connecting words; Type B—a string of endless clauses and phrases joined by connecting words.)

Fluent, correct structure:

Toby was a bear. He loved pancakes and didn't mind stealing them from our campsite. One day, he made off with more than 20!

Type A run-on:

Toby was a bear he loved pancakes and didn't mind stealing them from our campsite one day he made off with more than 20!

Type B run-on:

Toby was a bear and he loved pancakes and he didn't mind stealing them from our campsite so then one day he made off with more than 20!

Be sure all students recognize differences among these three ways of writing the same information. Ask for comments.

Teaching the Lesson

Knowing A from B

Make sure students read through the explanation of Type A and Type B run-ons. This should deepen their understanding. Then, expand on what they have learned from the introductory part of the lesson by asking them to write their own examples. They should begin with a three-sentence, fluent paragraph; then, they should add some Type A or Type B fluency problems. If you wish, have them read their problem passages to a partner.

Sharing an Example: *Dave at Night*

In this part of the lesson, students see run-ons at work, damaging the fluency in Gail Carson Levine's passage from *Dave at Night*. Make sure students read each passage aloud. Reading aloud underscores the fluency problem. Students should work with partners; one can read the Type A sample aloud, one the Type B. Remind students that it is easier to test the fluency of any passage if you *hear* it as well as see it.

Close Up

After reading each passage aloud and discussing it, students should take time to revise it. The first one has missing end punctuation and missing capitals; the second is overrun with connecting words. Read revisions aloud, and compare them to the problem texts students have revised.

Gail Carson Levine's Version— No Run-ons!

Be sure you or a volunteer reads Levine's passage aloud so that you can hear the difference in fluency. Then, ask students to rate the fluency in the simple chart that follows the paragraph. Discuss the results.

Stop the Runaway Run-on

Students must diagnose the nature of the problem in each passage and then solve it by revising the text. They can mark up the text to revise; it is not necessary to rewrite sample paragraphs.

A revision of Runaway Sentence #1 might read like this:

The sun was out for the first time in ages, and my brother and I were dying to play with the new lacrosse sticks we had bought with our own money. We quickly gathered all our equipment, got on our bikes, and rode down to the school. **Unfortunately,** *there were dozens of people there playing frisbee* **with their dogs.** *We decided to try a narrow strip of grass behind the playground.* **It** *was so muddy there, however, that we just decided to go home.*

(**Revision Strategies:** Adding capitals and periods, eliminating unneeded connecting words, using a pronoun— *It*—to avoid repetition, changing word order slightly, adding transitional words such as *Unfortunately.*)

A revision of Runaway Sentence #2 revision might read like this:

It was my job to walk the neighbors' dog whenever they decided to go away for the weekend. They paid me five dollars for each day. I had to walk their dog, Doony, twice each day, and also had to make sure she had food and water. If Doony even heard me rattling her leash, she would start to bark and jump. Even if she didn't hear the leash, I could make her bark by saying the word "walk" as if it were a question. It was really a pretty easy and fun job.

(**Revision Strategies:** Adding capitals and periods to separate sentences; eliminating unnecessary connecting words.)

Share and Compare

Revisions from the preceding part of the lesson should be shared aloud between partners. Discuss various strategies your students have used to improve fluency.

Extending the Lesson

- Share additional passages orally that either do or do not contain run-ons. See whether students can be sleuths with their ears, identifying run-ons they hear.

- Encourage students to scour their own writing for run-ons and to read it aloud to double-check.

From First to Last in Fluency

For use with pages 84–87 in the Student Traitbook

It's hard to appreciate a good song just by reading the lyrics. Certainly, some of the power and emotion would come through, but how much would be lost? To appreciate music, you must hear it. The same is true of writing. Fluent writing is best appreciated when eyes and ears are attuned to shifts in pace and rhythm. Reading aloud helps readers tune in, and eventually, given sufficient practice, they may hear the music of the text in their heads even when reading silently.

Objectives

Students will practice oral reading and listening skills to sharpen their acuity in assessing fluent text.

Skills Focus

- Identifying examples of strong fluency
- Ranking samples from least to most fluent
- Revising a nonfluent sample to improve fluency
- Reading aloud to help bring out the fluency of a text

Time Frame

Allow about 50 minutes for this lesson, excluding any extensions. You can divide the lesson into two parts, reviewing and ranking samples under "Rate the Writing First to Last" and reading, analyzing, and revising the sample under "Time to Revise." Students will also need time to share revisions orally with student partners.

Setting Up the Lesson

Responding to writing with their ears, not only their eyes, is uncomfortable for some students, especially if they have had little practice listening to stories or poems. A good warm-up, therefore, is to invite students to listen to various pieces and respond. If you like, begin with music. Choose a piece with lyrics, and just listen first. Then read the same lyrics aloud, with virtually no inflection at all. Insert some conjunctions where they do not belong. Breathe in the wrong places! Change the punctuation. In short, *eliminate* the fluency. Talk about the differences in the two readings. You can extend this warm-up lesson by reading two versions of the same poem—one a fluent interpretation, one not so fluent. Next, try a short sample of prose. Each time, ask students to listen for the contrast. Discuss the various elements (a review for many students) that contribute to fluency, such as variety, rhythmic flow, interpretive reading, enough connecting words—but not too many!

> *"I never wrote a word that I didn't hear as I read."*
>
> —Eudora Welty

Teaching the Lesson

Rate the Writing First to Last

Students should work with partners for this portion of the lesson. They will read three samples, A, B, and C, aloud and then rank them from least fluent to most fluent. In "Setting Up the Lesson," you have reminded them of the kinds of things they should look and listen for. Remind them one more time to respond with their ears, not just their eyes.

Fluency Rankings

In this brief assessment, students document their responses in writing. Most should see Sample C as the most fluent. It has great variety in sentence lengths and beginnings. It also has a natural, conversational sound, and it is easy to read aloud with inflection that helps bring out meaning. Sample A is in the middle. Though it is not difficult to read aloud, it does not display the variety of Sample C. Many sentences are the same length, and many begin similarly: with *I, You,* or *There.* Sample B is choppy by comparison and somewhat difficult to read aloud. The sentence fragments in this sample are not stylistically effective; in fact, they are awkward enough to slow a reader down a bit. (Ask students whether they had any difficulty reading this one aloud.) Students should indicate their rankings individually. Be sure they have reasons for their rankings. They may wish to mention features other than those just described.

Share and Compare

Here students compare their rankings with those of a partner. If they do not agree, encourage one partner or the other to read a passage aloud. Hearing it again may be all that's needed. Discuss results with the class as a whole, too. Did most of your students agree with our assessment?

Time to Revise

In this portion of the lesson, students apply what they have learned through oral reading, listening, and discussing of fluency in revising a nonfluent piece. They should first mark up the text in any way that is useful, such as crossing out words, filling in punctuation, adding transitional words or phrases, or changing word order. Then, each student should write out the revised version in the space provided, be prepared to share it with a partner, and reflect on the changes he or she has made.

Our suggested revision (students' revisions do not need to match):

Though I wanted to peer through the binoculars, the bright, hot sun made me squint and shield my eyes. I had been hoping to see a bald eagle so that I could tell my friends about it. When I looked back through the binoculars, I saw a flock of birds flying low over the lake, perhaps fishing. Then I saw its white head just as it dropped down and snagged a fish. It was a bald eagle, the symbol of our country.

Share and Compare

Be sure, in this sharing activity, that students remember to read their revisions aloud to each other. Readers should invite partners to comment on the revisions, noting the fluency and any strategies they hear in that revised version. Partners should also compare strategies. Share some samples (and strategies) with the class, too.

Extending the Lesson

- Share your own revision of the sample about the bald eagle. Invite students to comment on your fluency. Talk about specific strategies you used.

- Invite students to look for samples of fluent writing in anything they are currently reading. Samples could come from poems, novels, nonfiction writing, textbooks, magazines, newspapers, greeting cards, letters— anywhere at all! Gather as many as possible, from as many different kinds of sources as possible (You join the hunt, too!), and read them aloud. Post some samples. Make a fluency collage. (Samples can be as long as a paragraph or as short as a phrase.)

What Makes It Flow?

For use with pages 88–91 in the Student Traitbook

A good doctor may form an opinion about how well a patient is doing just by looking at him or her. Usually, though, doctors do not rely strictly on impressions. They do an analysis, taking a patient's temperature and blood pressure, listening to the heartbeat, and asking specific questions. Readers may sometimes want to do a similar kind of analysis of a text, just to see whether their impressions are borne out by the data. This lesson shows students how to do just that.

Objectives

Students will learn how to analyze writing for fluency, using a simple chart that breaks fluency down into some of its key components.

Skills Focus

- Responding to fluency by hearing text read aloud
- Reviewing a chart of fluency characteristics to see whether it bears out initial impressions
- Creating a similar chart based on a different piece of writing
- Summarizing in their own words what that chart shows about the fluency of a passage

Time Frame

Allow about 40 minutes for this lesson, excluding any extensions or the time required for students to locate a book for their own analysis.

Setting Up the Lesson

This lesson is about gathering data to back up an opinion, impression, or response. Help students understand that the purpose of the lesson is to illustrate the reasons behind the impression. We are not trying to suggest that students make charts for each piece of writing they encounter. Quite the opposite! In fact, the charts are likely to show that students can trust their impressions; there are real reasons for them!

Ask students to identify examples from everyday life in which data are used to back up impressions. One might be the medical example in the *Introduction* (Teacher Guide, page 88). Additional examples include weather, population growth, increases in traffic, weight loss or gain, athletic skills (such as time to run 100 meters), a baby's growth, the state of the economy, how well a student is doing in school, and so on. Talk about how data can support an impression. (Have students ever had the experience of believing one thing and then finding that the data tell another story?)

> *"Vigorous writing is concise."*
> —William Strunk

Teaching the Lesson

Sharing an Example: *In a Dark Wood*
Read this sample aloud as students listen. Then, ask for impressions. Though students will look at a careful point-by-point analysis of the piece, it is important to review impressions first so students see that the analysis actually supports those impressions. (At least that will be the case if they see the passage as fluent!)

Breaking Fluency Down
In this section of the lesson, students have a chance to review a chart that lists specific data on the *In a Dark Wood* passage: e.g., sentence lengths, sentence beginnings, transitional words. These specifics give us some clues about why this passage is fluent. For example, the variety in sentence lengths is stunning; author Michael Cadnum writes one sentence with only four words—and another with forty! That's quite an achievement in variety. Of course, we pick up that variety with our ears if we're good listeners. The analysis simply tells us, "Yes, the variety you thought you heard was real."

Discovering Fluency
This time around, students will work with a passage from a book they have selected. Remind them that the passage should be at least eight sentences long but not much longer, or the analysis will become tedious! After they have

filled out basic information on title, author, and page number, ask each student to complete the chart, using the one from the preceding section as a model. They should count carefully, but precise totals are less important than a picture of the variety shown in the passage.

Summing Up Your Analysis

We have provided a sample summary of *In a Dark Wood* to show how we might express in words what the data show. Students should write similar summaries on the basis of personal charts. The question is, of course, "Do the data show that you did indeed select a fluent passage?" In other words, the data should match the personal impression.

Share and Compare

Students should read passages aloud to partners to get their impressions. Is the fluency strong, fairly strong, or on the weak side? Then, share what the charts show.

Extending the Lesson

- Ask students to do a similar analysis on a passage they themselves have written. What does the chart show? Do the data support personal impressions of their own fluency?

- Also try analyzing a nonfluent piece identified by you or your students. What does the chart show this time around?

- Give students a topic, and ask them to write two versions—one fluent, one not so fluent. Then, ask students to analyze each and compare results. What do the charts show? Were students successful in creating a contrast?

- While we don't want our whole analysis of writing to be mathematical (opinions still count!), it might be fun to create a chart for another trait. Ask students to work with partners in creating similar analysis charts for any other trait. They should be prepared to present the chart and the thinking behind it.

- Is there anything about fluency that's just too hard to capture in a chart? If so, what? You might discuss this, or ask students to write a short, reflective paragraph responding to this question.

Sentence Fluency

Teacher's Guide pages 77, 168–179
Transparency numbers 17–20

Objective

Students will review and apply what they have learned about the trait of sentence fluency.

Reviewing Sentence Fluency

Review with students what they have learned about the trait of sentence fluency. Ask students to discuss what sentence fluency means and to explain why it is important in a piece of writing. Then ask them to recall the main points about sentence fluency that are discussed in Unit 5. Students' responses should include the following points:

- Vary sentence length to create interest.
- Rewrite awkward and run-on sentences.
- Revise text to make it fluent.
- Check for smoothness and flow.

Applying Sentence Fluency

To help students apply what they have learned about the trait of sentence fluency, distribute copies of the Student Rubric for Sentence Fluency on page 77 of this Teacher's Guide. Students will use these to score one or more of the sample papers that begin on page 116. The papers for sentence fluency are also on overhead transparencies 17–20.

Before students score the papers, explain that a rubric is a grading system to determine the score a piece of writing should receive for a particular trait. Preview the Student Rubric for Sentence Fluency, pointing out that a paper that reads smoothly receives a score of 6 and a paper that does not read at all smoothly receives a score of 1. Tell students to read the rubric and then read the paper to be scored. Then tell them to look at the paper and rubric together to determine the score the paper should receive. Encourage students to make notes on each paper to help them score it. For example, they might underline repetitive sentence beginnings or put an X next to each run-on sentence.

Overview

Editors' tools include not only such basics as a sharp pencil, a good dictionary, and a handbook, but more personal things as well. For example, a good editor needs to develop an editor's eye and an editor's ear in order to weed out every mistake hiding within the text. Editors also need a code— a set of symbols with which to mark the text for editing—and a personal checklist to keep track of hard-to-remember conventional rules.

The focus of the instruction in this unit will be

- understanding the differences between revising and editing.
- recognizing and applying ten editor's marks in editing text.
- creating a personalized editing checklist.

Conventions: *A Definition*

The trait of conventions includes anything a copy editor would deal with: spelling, punctuation, usage and grammar, capitalization, and indentation (or other indicators of paragraphing, such as spacing). Conventions can also include presentation on the page: general layout, headings and subheadings, citations, use of white space, formatting, use of fonts for stylistic effect, and incorporation of charts, graphs, illustrations, and so on into the text. While we will not deal with this aspect of conventions, it is entirely appropriate to consider them in assessing classroom work for which layout is critical: A writer who can handle many conventions well, and who can find and correct many errors in a draft, has met our goals for this trait.

The Unit at a Glance

The following lessons in the Teacher's Guide and practice exercises in the Student Traitbook will help develop an understanding of the trait of conventions. The Unit Summary provides an opportunity to practice evaluating papers for the trait of conventions.

Unit Overview: Conventions

Teacher's Guide pages 92–96

The unique features of the trait of conventions are presented along with a rubric and a list of recommended resources for teaching conventions.

Lesson 21: Revising, Editing, or "Revisediting"?

Teacher's Guide pages 97–99
Student Traitbook pages 92–96

Students will learn to distinguish between revising (making major structural or conceptual changes) and editing (correcting errors to increase clarity).

Lesson 22: The Editor's Code

Teacher's Guide pages 100–103
Student Traitbook pages 97–100

In this lesson, students are introduced to and use ten editor's marks.

Lesson 23: Eyes, Ears, Rules, and Tools

Teacher's Guide pages 104–107
Student Traitbook pages 101–103

Many editors *hear* errors their eyes miss. In this lesson, students track down errors and apply editing marks.

Lesson 24: A Personalized Checklist

Teacher's Guide pages 108–111
Student Traitbook pages 104–106

One person's easy-to-remember conventional rule is another person's nemesis! Students will make a personalized checklist.

Unit Summary: Conventions

Teacher's Guide page 112
Overhead Numbers 21–24

Use the student rubric on page 95 and the activities in the Summary to practice assessing writing for the trait of conventions. Remember, 6-point rubrics, along with rationales for scores on sample papers, appear in the Appendix of this Teacher's Guide, pages 192–214.

Teacher Rubric for Conventions

6
- Only the pickiest editors will spot the remaining errors. Their impact on the text is insignificant.
- The writer uses conventions skillfully to bring out meaning and/or voice.
- The writer shows control over a wide range of conventions for this grade level.
- This piece is ready to publish.

5
- A few errors are noticeable if you hunt for them. None affect clarity.
- The writer often uses conventions to enhance meaning or voice.
- The writer shows control over numerous conventions appropriate for grade level.
- This piece is ready to publish with minor touch-ups.

4
- Errors are noticeable, but they do not impair meaning or significantly slow a reader down.
- The writer uses conventions with enough skill to make the text quite readable.
- The writer shows control over many conventions appropriate for grade level.
- A good once-over is needed prior to publication.

3
- Noticeable, distracting errors begin to slow a reader down, though it is still possible to figure out the message.
- Though many things are done correctly, errors are sufficiently serious that they affect readability.
- The writer knows some conventions—but is not yet in control.
- Thorough, careful editing is needed prior to publication.

2
- Numerous errors make reading a chore.
- Though a few things are done correctly, serious errors impair readability.
- This writer appears to know a few conventions but is not in control of them.
- Line-by-line editing is required prior to publication.

1
- Serious, frequent errors make this text hard to read.
- The reader must search to find things done correctly.
- This writer does not appear in control of many conventions appropriate for this grade level.
- Careful, word-by-word editing is required for publication.

Student Rubric for Conventions

6
- You have to be really picky to find any errors in my paper!
- I used conventions to make my message clear and to bring out the voice.
- I thoroughly edited this paper and feel confident that I found and corrected all errors.
- I looked and listened for mistakes more than once. This is ready to publish.

5
- You might find a few errors—but you will really have to hunt for them!
- I think my conventions help make my message clear.
- I checked my paper over pretty thoroughly, and I am sure I corrected the major errors.
- I looked and listened for mistakes. I might have missed some small things. It's almost ready to publish, though.

4
- You will probably notice some errors. I need to edit more carefully.
- My message is still clear, I think.
- Though I did check it over quickly, I should probably take one more look.
- This paper still needs careful editing before it's ready to publish.

3
- I have too many errors. This draft is still pretty rough!
- I did *some* things correctly. Still—I'm not sure my message is always clear.
- Just looking the paper over, I see enough errors in spelling, punctuation, or grammar to slow a reader down.
- This could use *a lot* of editing. It is not ready to publish.

2
- I have a lot of errors! Wow! This is hard to read.
- I did *a few* things correctly, but mistakes get in the way of my message.
- The errors in spelling, punctuation, and grammar will definitely slow a reader down.
- I need to read this aloud and edit it line by line before I publish it.

1
- I made so many mistakes I can hardly read this myself.
- It is hard to find things done correctly or even to tell what my message is.
- I see many errors—and many kinds of errors—here.
- I need to read this aloud, work with a partner, and edit my paper word by word before I publish it.

Recommended Books for Teaching Conventions

Though we do recommend the use of the handbook *Write Source 2000* (see annotation below), no extended book list is included with these lessons because you can use any book to help teach conventions. We do recommend that you use sections from students' favorite books to talk about writers' skills in using conventions and about how conventions help bring out meaning. Commas and semicolons indicate pauses in thought, for instance, while quotation marks indicate speech. Dashes, italics, boldface type, or ellipses may influence the way a reader "hears" or interprets a passage. As always, it is the meaning behind the convention that counts. As you share published text, be sure to notice the following:

- Various conventions authors have used to make meaning clear
- Authors' use of conventions to enhance voice
- Any conventions that may be new to students
- Any conventions students would change on the basis of personal style
- Any errors (There are few in published books, but they do appear—and errors are common in newspapers, advertisements, mailings, or any publication for which the review/editing process is rapid.)

You will also find numerous lessons, strategies, explanations, and tips to help students with conventions in this Great Source handbook:

Sebranek, Patrick, Dave Kemper, and Verne Meyer. *Write Source 2000.* 1999. Wilmington, MA: Great Source Education Group, Inc. A handbook in a class by itself. Helpful, user-friendly information on agreement, modifiers, parts of speech, conventional problems of all kinds, revising and editing, checklists, usage, problem words, proofreading, punctuation, spelling, editing marks, citations and bibliographies, and other terms and concepts related to conventions. Your students will find it invaluable!

More Ideas

Looking for more ideas on using literature to teach the trait of conventions? We recommend *Books, Lessons, Ideas for Teaching the Six Traits: Writing at Middle and High School,* published by Great Source. Compiled and annotated by Vicki Spandel. For information, please phone 800-289-4490.

Revising, Editing, or "Revisediting"?

For use with pages 92–96 in the Student Traitbook

Revising and editing are related parts of the writing process, but they involve different kinds of changes to text. Revision is big and sweeping and may involve adding or deleting information, moving pieces of text around, and general reworking or reshaping of ideas. Editing, on the other hand, is the attention to detail.

Objectives

Students will deepen their understanding of revising and editing, will recognize samples of each (given text that has been altered), and will create personal definitions for *revising* and *editing*.

Skills Focus

- Reviewing personal writing to identify strategies used in revising and editing
- Creating personal definitions for these parts of the writing process
- Classifying specific changes as revising or editing
- Analyzing altered text to determine whether the changes represent revising or editing

Time Frame

Allow about 30 minutes for this lesson.

Setting Up the Lesson

The purpose of this lesson is to help students understand the differences between revising and editing. Revision is BIG and involves major changes to text that come from the writer's evolving thinking about a topic. In revising, a writer may rearrange information, add details, say things in a new way, or delete portions of text. Editing, on the other hand—while equally important—requires a different kind of change: namely, the correction of errors in spelling, punctuation, grammar, and so on. It is helpful to students to share a few analogies. For example, adding a room to a house would be a kind of "revising"; washing the dishes would be "editing." See how many similar examples from real life your students can come up with: for example,

Salting the soup would be . . .

Remodeling the kitchen would be . . .

Dusting the furniture would be . . .

Repapering the walls would be . . .

Teaching the Lesson

Moving Toward a Definition

Students should complete each part of this section on their own prior to discussing their thinking with a partner. The two samples are very different and should readily clarify the distinction between revising and editing. In Sample 1, the writer changes wording, adds detail, rearranges information, reworks sentence structure to build fluency, and adds voice. These changes signify revision. In Sample 2, the writer makes no changes in content, organization, voice, or wording. The writer does, however, make corrections. This is a good example of editing.

Share and Compare

Make sure students understand the differences between Samples 1 and 2 before going on. They can share with partners first and then extend the discussion to the class as a whole.

Revising or Editing?

This time around, students do not see the actual changes to the text. Instead, they are given five possible changes and asked to classify each as revision or editing. We classify them as follows:

1. Revising (Adding detail is a significant change.)

2. Editing (Inserting a comma is a small correction.)

3. Revising (Moving text is a major change.)

4. Revising (Varying sentence beginnings calls for a change in word choice as well as attention to fluency and the links between ideas.)

5. Editing (This is a spelling correction.)

Students should check responses with partners first and then discuss their choices with the class as a whole. In most cases, you should get unanimous agreement. If you do not, let both sides be heard and ask the class to vote. Remember—individual examples are not important here. What counts is students' understanding of revising and editing.

Time to Define

In this closing activity, students create a personal definition for revising and editing that can be shared with a partner and with the class.

Extending the Lesson

• Ask students to create additional analogies that define revising and editing. Post these or share them aloud.

• Invite some creative role-playing. Ask one student to play the part of "Editing" and another to play the part of "Revising." Suppose they met for lunch or while waiting for the bus. What might they have to say to each other? Would they be friends? Would they get into an argument? Think creatively on this one.

The Editor's Code

For use with pages 97–100 in the Student Traitbook

Editors use their own special code—a set of editor's symbols—for marking up text. Knowing and using these symbols empowers your young editors to work as a professional would, marking the text to signify the kinds of changes needed to make that text correct. This lesson introduces students to ten editor's marks, some of which may be familiar from previous editing practice or work with the trait of conventions.

Objectives

Students will learn (or review) ten editor's symbols and will begin working with those symbols in editing faulty text.

Skills Focus

- Identifying ten editor's marks
- Learning to "read" each mark
- Using the editing marks to indicate faulty text

Time Frame

Allow about 55 minutes for this lesson, excluding any extensions. You can divide the lesson into two parts, if you wish. In Part 1 of the lesson (25 minutes), review the chart of editing marks. Then complete the section called "Warming Up to the Code," and discuss results to ensure that all students are "reading" the marks the same way. In Part 2 of the lesson (30 minutes), complete the section called "Using the Code to Send a Message," in which students mark the text *Olympic Skating* for editing. Allow time for students to compare results with a partner.

Setting Up the Lesson

Before students look at the chart of editing marks, see how much they already know. You might write a delete symbol ⌒ on the overhead. Ask what it is and what it is used for. Try a caret ∧, and ask the same thing. Try the symbols for capitalization ≡, new paragraph ¶, or period ⊙. In each case, see how many students know the mark already; then ask how many use it in their own editing. Now that you've tested their knowledge, it's time to move on to a review of the chart.

> *In baseball you only get three swings and you're out. In rewriting, you get almost as many swings as you want and you know, sooner or later, you'll hit the ball.*
>
> —Neil Simon

Teaching the Lesson

The Power of Ten

Extend the discussion you've already had in "Setting Up the Lesson" by reviewing the chart, mark by mark. Encourage questions. If any mark is confusing, use the overhead projector or board to provide an additional example. It is also helpful if students write out their own examples and practice using marks appropriately as you go along. (This is just a scratch paper exercise; you do not need to collect or assess it.)

Warming Up to the Code

In this part of the lesson, students practice "reading" copy editor's marks to make sure they know what each one means. They will not need to correct the text or make any changes. Rather, the purpose here is to interpret the editor's intent. Students should look at each example, see whether they can tell what directions the editor's marks provide and then briefly note those directions in the space provided. Remind them to look back at the chart of editing marks at any time during this exercise. When they finish, they should share with a partner. Then, review each of the three examples to be sure everyone is on track. (**HINT:** You may wish to put these samples on the overhead so you can point to various marks as you discuss them.) Here are the three samples with corrections made and marked in boldface:

Sample 1 (**two** paragraphs)
   "**P**lease stop bothering me!" Hannah yelled.

   "**W**hat are you going to do, tell Dad**?**" asked her sister.

Sample 2 (**one** paragraph)
   I think rainy days [Delete second "days"] are the best. [No new paragraph] When it rains, I **l**ike to go out and **jump** in puddles**,** plug up the

street drain, and float sticks in front
of the neighbor's **h**ouse.

Sample 3
I'll mow the **lawn** tomorrow [delete
comma] if **it** doesn't rain.

Using the Code to Send a Message
This is the flip side of the coin. Here,
instead of reading and decoding marks
inserted by another editor, students
become the editors. They should read
through the passage titled "Olympic
Skating" first—just to get an idea of the
number and kinds of errors the text
contains. Then, ask students to edit the
passage using the chart of editing marks
for reference and inserting marks as
necessary. They do not need to rewrite
the paragraph. Here is the sample with
editor's marks correctly placed:

one of my favorite events in in the

olympics is speed skating. In my mind,
                                    than
it is so much better figure skating,

which is my sisters favorite event. My

sister and I were arguing about which

was better. She said, Who cares about

how fast you go! Besides, i like the

music and the the Costumes." "Music

and costumes! I yelled. "Speed skaters

go so fast they have to wear helmets."

She just doesnt get it. With the helmets,

the long-bladed skates, the aerodynamic

suits, and the speed, what could be

better? I guess we'll have to agree to

disagree about the skating, or see

whether we can can make brother-sister

arguing an olympic event.

Code Check
In this final portion of the lesson, each
student should compare his or her
editing with that of a partner and then
with your own edited version from
the Teacher's Guide. Again, encourage
students to raise questions about any
marks or corrections they missed or do
not understand. You may wish to tally
how many students caught all or
most of the errors we marked, how
many caught at least half, and so on.
Did anyone find additional errors?
Sometimes students become a little
over-zealous and mark changes that are
not actually corrections but stylistic
alterations. If this happens, be sure you
take time to discuss the difference!

Extending the Lesson

• Create a poster-sized chart of editing
  marks to put on your wall for handy
  reference. Feel free to add other
  marks that your students know. (See
  the back inside cover of *Write Source
  2000* for ideas; you can also check a
  dictionary under *proofreader's marks*.)

- Ask students who know additional marks (beyond the ten on the chart) to share them with the rest of the class.

- Find or create additional faulty passages that students can use to practice their editing skills. Student writing works well, but it is often helpful if you can take time to write passages.

- Brainstorm ideas for making editing easier: for example, double-spacing rough drafts, having the chart of editing marks handy, or reading text more than once.

- Invite students to hunt for errors in *any* text they read. They can bring in examples and mark them as an editor would. Post these mini-editing samples.

- Ask students in teams to create short, faulty passages and then exchange passages with partners. The partners should use editor's symbols to make corrections and then check with the original writer to see whether they've found all the errors.

- Invite students to peruse writing from their folders. They should select a piece that has not yet been edited, go through it carefully, and mark at least five items for correction. Can't find five? Take one more look, read aloud, and then have a partner double-check to be sure!

Eyes, Ears, Rules, and Tools

For use with pages 101–103 in the Student Traitbook

Editors need tools to do a good job. We're not talking about saws and hammers—or even a sharp pencil (though that's a help). In this lesson, the focus is on personalizing the editor's toolkit to include a sharp editor's eye, good listening skills, knowledge of editor's symbols, and the speed that comes only with lots of practice.

Objectives

Students will expand their understanding of editor's symbols from Lesson 22 by editing more challenging text.

Skills Focus

- Identifying conventional errors in faulty text
- Counting errors as a way of checking proficiency
- Using editing symbols to indicate faulty text
- Developing increasing confidence as an editor

Time Frame

Allow about 70 minutes for this lesson, excluding any extensions. You can divide the lesson into two parts, if you wish. In Part 1 (30 minutes), ask students to review and edit the sample about Wisconsin under "Getting Focused." They will also need time for partners to compare results and time to check their work against your corrected copy. In Part 2 (40 minutes), have them review and edit the slightly longer sample under "A Job for the Editor." Again, allow time for comparison with partners' work and a check against your corrected sample from the Teacher's Guide.

Setting Up the Lesson

This lesson is a lot like *Where's Waldo?*—only this time around, the question is, "Where's the error?" Give students a chance to warm up on some short passages you write on the overhead. See how quickly they can spot an error, and then tell you what editorial symbol to insert. Start with something very simple, such as this sentence that has no period:

Harriet hated her new hat

Correct it:

Harriet hated her new hat⊙

Now try something a little more difficult, such as this sentence with a missing word:

It was hot and sticky in the town Bloomville.

And again, correct it:

It was hot and sticky in the town^of Bloomville.

Do three or four examples—or as many as you need until you think students are warmed up and ready for a more difficult task.

Teaching the Lesson

Getting Focused

Students should complete this portion of the lesson individually. As they work on editing this passage about weather,

encourage them to (1) read the passage aloud at least once, (2) refer to the chart of symbols to remind themselves which symbols go with which corrections, and (3) read through the passage more than one time, because it is very easy to miss errors. When students are finished, they should fill in the blanks to show the number and kinds of errors they found.

Have students compare their editing symbols with partners. When the partners have finished their discussions, share your corrected version from the Teacher's Guide. You can do this in one of two ways: (1) simply share the corrections provided, going through the passage error by error, or (2) put an unedited copy of the text on the overhead, and ask students to tell you, error by error, what changes to make. (Of course, you may need to coach them just a bit to make sure they do not miss anything or overcorrect!) Following is a corrected version of the Wisconsin passage, with editor's symbols inserted for you:

I'm from Wisconsin, where there are̶ are real winters with lots of snow͵ice͵and below-zero temperatures͗when I moved to oregon, I had to laugh the first time it snowed. I wouldnt even have called it snow͵ but everyone around here ^was all excited. All the local news people put on these Parkas with their channel number and logo. "Stay tuned to News 5 for all the traffic and weather updates as we cover Winter Storm 2002," the announcer said very seriously. ¶ "Winter storm! Ha!" my brother and I yelled back at the the TV. These people don't know what a winter storm really is.

A Job for the Editor

This is more editing practice but with a slightly longer passage, so the task is more challenging and takes more time. Follow the same procedures as before, asking each student to work alone before comparing notes with a partner. Again, encourage students to read aloud, read the passage more than once, and refer to the editing chart of symbols as necessary.

Again, students should compare with partners first, checking the number and the kinds of errors each found. Encourage students to think of themselves as an editing team; any error one misses, the other should find. Together, they should find them all (or close to it!).

Give students one final look at the text prior to sharing your corrected version. Again, we encourage you to elicit their feedback first before giving them the answers. See what they found, what they corrected. Then, let them check their corrections against your own corrected text from the Teacher's Guide. Do students agree on the errors as you go along? Be sure to invite questions on anything that is unclear! Following is an edited version of the neighborhood passage with symbols inserted:

About a Year ago, a new high school was was built in the neighborhood. It's within walking distance of my house, which is good. The problem is all the extra traffic that now comes through our neighborhood. There are a lot more cars than there used to be, and most of them are driven by younger drivers. This makes my parents nervous. It seems as if there are more cars going too fast and fewer cars actually stopping at the intersection near our house. "Mina," my father said to me last night, "you've got to be extra careful crossing the street and riding your bike. "Trust me," i told him, "I want to live to be a seventh grader."

The neighbors got together at the high school for a meeting with people from the city, the police department, and from the school. they came ~~up~~ up with a plan to put in traffic speed bumps to slow down the **traffic**. Now, all we have to do is get everyone in the neighborhood to agree to the plan.

Extending the Lesson

- Practice builds confidence. Ask students to design their own editing lessons. Have them enter 10 or fewer sentences into a word processor and then build in a few errors. They should not get carried away, or their lessons will be too difficult! Six to ten errors are enough. They should, however, try for variety to make the task challenging. Copies can be made for classmates to use for practice. Final editing should be compared to the author's original.

- Some of your students probably rate themselves as highly confident editors, some as still "a little shaky." What makes the difference?

Brainstorm a list of things an editor can do to build confidence.

- Invite students to do individual or team mini-lessons in editing by writing one sentence on the overhead that contains two to three errors. See how quickly classmates can spot and correct those errors. If this becomes too easy, let them write two or three sentences and put a maximum of four errors in each sentence. Now you're editing! (A mini-lesson like this takes from five to twelve minutes, depending on the length and complexity of the corrections.) Don't forget this no-exceptions rule: Students conducting the mini-lesson must know where the errors are and must know the right symbols to use to correct them!

A Personalized Checklist

For use with pages 104–106 in the Student Traitbook

One editor may be a crackerjack speller but may forget to indent for paragraphs. Another is a paragraphing maniac but can't seem to recall the rules on commas. When it comes to conventions, we all have our strengths and our pitfalls. A personalized checklist simply serves as a handy reminder of those errors most likely to cause each of us trouble. Like any good list, it says, "Hey, don't forget this . . ."

Objectives

Students will review their own writing, looking for repeated errors or other editorial problems and will build a personalized checklist based on their findings.

Skills Focus

- Reviewing personal writing
- Honestly analyzing editorial problems
- Understanding how a checklist can help an editor improve his or her skills

Time Frame

Allow about 35 minutes for this lesson, excluding any extensions. Each student will need time to review his or her personal writing (more than a single paper is necessary to get the full value of the lesson), to compile a list of editing problems, and to compare it with a partner's.

Setting Up the Lesson

Remind students that a checklist works only if it is an honest reflection of the writer's or editor's true skills—and it is OK not to be perfect! It is helpful to begin by naming just one thing each person could improve when it comes to editing. (That's not too risky or revealing—after all, it's just one thing.) You start. What's your major downfall? Spelling? Punctuation? Paragraphing? Commas, semicolons, dashes—what? Name it; then encourage your students to do the same as you go around the room. Each person should name only one trouble spot; no details (or long stories of woe!) are needed—just a quick identification of the problem (ten seconds per person).

Teaching the Lesson

An Honest Look in the Writer's Mirror

Time to get more serious—and more detailed. The warm-up may have helped students (as they listened to you and their classmates) think of some problems they'd forgotten. Now they can confirm those suspicions by reviewing their own work. They should look carefully through three or four papers. Fewer may not provide enough substance for a good analysis; more may get too cumbersome and time consuming. As students go through their work, encourage them to make

notes and to use check marks to indicate problems that seem to come up a lot. Remind them that this is *not* a time for making corrections; rather, they should go quickly through the text, getting an idea of what is there. Honesty is the key. Good editors dare to admit that they need to improve in certain areas. They dare to look in the mirror!

Once they have completed their reviews and made a few notes, they should write the key problems on the list provided. It is not necessary to fill in all eight blanks, but if a writer/editor has fewer than four items listed, ask whether he or she has done a thorough review!

Share and Compare

This is the time for students to compare lists and to note which items come up for both partners. There will usually be at least one. Reassure students that this happens because some things (like remembering quotation marks or spelling hard words) are difficult for many people.

Create a class editing checklist from the students' individual checklists. The list of common problems does two things. First, it reinforces the notion that students are not alone in finding certain editing tasks difficult. Second, it builds a sense of teamwork. Editing teams can work together to identify and solve problems. This does not mean that some students will turn their work over to others. Each writer should be his or her own editor. It does mean, however, that students can help one another by modeling, coaching, or rechecking a passage to make sure all errors have been found.

The Incredible Shrinking List

This portion of the lesson cannot be completed in any one class period. It's an ongoing task. The idea is for students to use their lists efficiently in improving as editors. When a problem has not shown up for a while (not in the last three papers a student has produced), the student can check it off the list. Of course, if it crops up again, it returns to the list. Similarly, if a new problem arises, the student should add it to the list. The list should be ever-changing, as editing problems are targeted and resolved.

Extending the Lesson

- From your brainstormed list, identify an editing "Problem of the Week." If you like, have some fun with this, and let one of your students role-play this problem while other students ask questions: *Where do you like to hang out? What makes you so pesky? What could we do to get rid of you? What kinds of writers do you like to pick on?* and so on. Target this "Problem of the Week" by asking ALL students to be on editorial lookout duty. Whatever else goes wrong editorially in students' work, that problem will not show up!

- You have already brainstormed a list of problems. Why not look on the bright side and brainstorm a list of things your student editors believe they're good at? Post it, add to it, and change it as your editing team grows stronger.

- Identify students who specialize in correcting one particular kind of editing problem: spelling, punctuation, dialogue, paragraphing, and so on. During editing time in your class, invite those students to set up a consultation area to help other students with those specific problems. This does NOT mean they will do all the editing for other students. It simply provides an opportunity to offer *one kind* of advice.

- The Academy of Motion Picture Arts and Sciences gives Oscars for exceptional performance in films. Why not create your own Academy of Fine Editorial Arts and brainstorm a list of creative awards (come up with a name like Oscar) you can give: for example, Most Improved Title, Best Control Over Commas, Best Editing of a First Paragraph. Nominees would be named by partners (with the partner's permission), who would explain the editor's achievement. It's perfectly fair for editing partners to invent new categories to match any outstanding editing achievement (no matter how small!).

- Continue using the personal checklists. From time to time, ask students to update these. Then do a class survey to see what new problems have arisen or which editing difficulties have been resolved. Discuss results.

ConVentions

Teacher's Guide pages 95, 180–191
Transparency numbers 21–24

Objective

Students will review and apply what they have learned about the trait of conventions.

Reviewing ConVentions

Review with students what they have learned about the trait of conventions. Ask students to discuss what conventions are and to explain why they are important in a piece of writing. Then ask them to recall the main points about conventions that are discussed in Unit 6. Students' responses should include the following points:

- Understand the difference between revising and editing.
- Use editor's symbols correctly to mark errors.
- Read aloud to hear errors.
- Make a personal editing checklist.

Applying ConVentions

To help students apply what they have learned about the trait of conventions, distribute copies of the Student Rubric for Conventions on page 95 of this Teacher's Guide. Students will use these to score one or more of the sample papers that begin on page 116. The papers for conventions are also on overhead transparencies 21–24.

Before students score the papers, explain that a rubric is a grading system to determine the score a piece of writing should receive for a particular trait. Preview the Student Rubric for Conventions, pointing out that a paper very strong in conventions receives a score of 6 and a paper very weak in conventions receives a score of 1. Tell students to read the rubric and then read the paper to be scored. Then tell them to look at the paper and rubric together to determine the score the paper should receive. Encourage students to make notes on each paper to help them score it. For example, they might use editor's marks to note errors.

The two closure activities in this section are designed for students who have had a chance to work with all six traits of writing. This closure section should not be thought of as a test but rather as a reminder and review as well as a chance to pull all the traits together.

Wrap-up Activity 1 should take about 15 minutes. Activity 2 has four writing samples. Each sample can be used for an individual or class activity. Allow about 10 minutes per sample to give students time to read the sample, discuss it with a partner, and determine the main problem. Finally, allow several minutes for class discussion.

Wrap-up Activity 1

EgoMania

For use with Student Traitbook pages 107–108

In this activity, the six traits are represented as characters with egos as big as the sky. Each trait, in turn, brags about the importance of its role in good writing. Each student's task is to see whether he or she can match the name of the trait with the egotistical description the trait "character" provides.

After students have completed their work, have each student discuss his or her responses with a partner. Then discuss the answers as a group.

Answers: 1. Conventions 2. Voice 3. Organization 4. Word Choice 5. Sentence Fluency 6. Ideas

Making a Diagnosis

For use with Student Traitbook pages 109–112

In order to revise effectively, a writer must read a piece of writing and identify the writing problems. Making such a diagnosis is the first step toward **revision.**

After students have made their decisions, discuss the samples with the class. If any students disagree with a diagnosis, let them explain why they disagree. Students may find additional problems. That's fine, as long as they support each diagnosis.

Response and Rationale for Sample 1

The answer should be **d, Word Choice.** The problem with this text is that the writer repeats *great* and *weird* and uses such vague language that it is hard to picture anything about the cake baking or the party itself. The paper has focus, so there is no real problem with ideas—other than some weakness in detail, which is connected to the weakness in word choice. The conventions are fine, so answer **b** does not make sense. Although the writing is less than exciting, it is organized, so answer **c** does not make sense either.

Response and Rationale for Sample 2

The answer should be **c, Sentence Fluency.** The main problem with this text is that the sentences are either run-ons (the first, fourth, and sixth "sentences" are examples), or they are so short and choppy that they break up the flow of the writing. Both problems make this text difficult to read aloud with any kind of grace. The main idea is clear. The organization is fine, too, and the paper has a definite lead and conclusion. Therefore, answers **a** and **b** do not apply. In addition, the paper has voice, especially when the writer talks about landing face-first in the snow and the reactions of his or her friends, so answer **d** is not appropriate either.

Response and Rationale for Sample 3

The main problem is **a, Voice.** The writer seems to have little or no engagement with the topic. It's a wonder he or she can stay awake long enough to write this much. "I forget where it was. We walked around and stuff . . ." Where's the energy? Where's the excitement or connection with the audience? The paper does not have run-ons, and most sentences begin quite differently, so answer **b** is not appropriate. The conventions are fine, so answer **c** does not apply. The organization could use some work, but simply moving things around will not make this a strong piece of writing.

Response and Rationale for Sample 4

The main problem with this text is the abrupt conclusion, so answer **c, Organization,** is the best choice. "Like he would know!" has a certain zip to it, but it does not leave the reader with a sense of finality or resolution. Is this behavior going to keep up? Will Brandon write the paper— or will that turn into another of his behavioral disasters? The word choice is excellent; count the verbs! Answer **a** makes no sense. The ideas are very clear and detailed; we can picture Brandon's escapades perfectly, so answer **b** is not appropriate either. Certainly this piece resounds with voice. It asks to be read aloud. Answer **d** does not work. The only serious problem is the hasty conclusion.

Extensions

- Have each student write a letter that tells why it is important that a piece of writing be strong in the six traits. Work with students to make notes about what to say in their letters. Students can then use these notes as they write their letters.

- Invite volunteers to lead a scoring discussion on any Sample Paper for **all six traits.** Have students score the paper prior to class and make a list of questions to ask. Refer to the poster for either the 6-point rubric or the 5-point rubric.

Contents

Sample Papers

Sample Papers: Introduction

The purpose of the Sample Papers is to help students view each trait as a whole. By learning to evaluate a piece of writing, students will become better revisers and writers. This Sample Papers section contains copymasters of Sample Papers. There are four Sample Papers for each trait, twenty-four papers in all. Each sample paper is also on an overhead transparency. For each trait, you will find two fairly strong papers and two weaker (in process) papers. The Teacher's Guide will give you suggested scores and a rationale for a particular perspective on every paper.

Using the Sample Papers

You can use each paper alone, for which you need to allow about 20 minutes (the approximate time required to read, score, and discuss one paper). As an alternative, you can use the papers in pairs, in which case you need to allow at least 40 minutes. You must decide whether your students can focus their attention for such an extended discussion. If you decide to use papers in pairs, we strongly recommend that you select one strong paper and one weak paper to provide contrast.

It is important to present the traits in the order in which they appear in the Student Traitbook and in the Teacher's Guide. You may, however, present the four papers for an individual trait in any order you wish. Read in advance all four papers for the trait at hand, and decide how you will present them. This will also give you time to become familiar with the papers before discussing them with your class.

In advance

- Read the paper aloud to *yourself* so you know it well and feel prepared to share it with students.

- Make a copy of the appropriate student rubric and the sample paper for each student.

At the time of the lesson

- Remind students about key points they should be looking or listening for in response to a particular paper (trait). Keep this list *short.* (Tips are given in your Teacher's Guide for each paper.)

- Read the paper aloud to your students, using as much inflection as the text allows. One paper may have very strong voice, and another may have a very weak voice. Be enthusiastic, but don't try to "invent" voice where it does not exist. (about 1–2 minutes)

- Have students reflect on the relative strengths or weaknesses of a paper. (about 4–5 minutes)

- Ask students to state *in writing* the score a paper should receive for a given trait before talking to other students. Do not share your own opinion yet. (1 minute)

- If you use hard copies of the papers, you may wish to ask students to perform simple tasks such as underlining favorite words or circling overused words. Allow time for this before discussing the paper. (1–2 minutes)

- Ask students to compare responses with a partner. Have them answer a question such as, "Why do you think this paper is strong in ideas?" (about 3–4 minutes)

- Lead a full-class discussion. Ask students to justify their decisions: Why did they think the paper was strong or weak? Suggested questions for each paper are provided in your Teacher's Guide. (5 minutes or less)

- End by sharing your own response to the paper. You should do this only once, after students have finished giving their responses, and you should be open to changing your mind or allowing students to disagree. You may wish to refer to the *Rationale* for the paper at hand (which provides reasons for viewing a paper as strong or weak) in formulating your own response. (1 minute)

Sample Papers

IDEAS

Paper 1: How to Drive Your Teacher Crazy (Score: 4)*
Paper 2: Boomer (Score: 6)
Paper 3: Dolly (Score: 3)
Paper 4: Least Favorite Chore (Score: 2)

ORGANIZATION

Paper 5: How to Snowboard (Score: 4)
Paper 6: A Day to Remember (Score: 1)
Paper 7: Grizzly Bears (Score: 6)
Paper 8: Getting Stitches (Score: 2)

VOICE

Paper 9: Lose the Hiccups (Score: 6)
Paper 10: Climbing Rocket Butte (Score: 3)
Paper 11: Parking the Car with Dad (Score: 5)
Paper 12: Too Much Television (Score: 1)

WORD CHOICE

Paper 13: Pasta, Pasta, Pasta! (Score: 5)
Paper 14: Autumn—My Favorite Season! (Score: 3)
Paper 15: Desert Creatures (Score: 6)
Paper 16: Something I Learned to Do (Score: 2)

SENTENCE FLUENCY

Paper 17: Dinosaurs in the Movies (Score: 2)
Paper 18: Sneezing Etiquette (Score: 6)
Paper 19: Seals (Score: 3)
Paper 20: Birthday Gift (Score: 5)

CONVENTIONS

Paper 21: Kites (Score: 5)
Paper 22: Traffic Flow (Score: 2)
Paper 23: I Can't Believe It! (Score: 1)
Paper 24: I Could Swim Forever (Score: 6)

*See the appendix, beginning on page 192, for using a 5-point rubric.

Sample Paper 1: How to Drive Your Teacher Crazy

Objective

Students will learn that clear supporting details add interest and enhance the main idea.

Materials

Student Rubric for Ideas (Teacher's Guide page 5)

Sample Paper 1: How to Drive Your Teacher Crazy (Teacher's Guide page 122 and/or Transparency 1)

Scoring the Paper

1. Give each student a copy of the sample paper and the Student Rubric for Ideas. Use the rubric to focus students' attention on the key features of the trait of IDEAS—a strong main main idea and details that support it. Review that a detail is important or interesting information.

2. Have students think about these questions as they listen to you read the paper: *Does this writer stay focused on the main topic (annoying your teacher)? Does the writer tell us enough details to fully describe how to drive your teacher crazy?*

3. Ask students to score the paper *individually,* using the rubric. They should mark their scores in writing, putting an **X** in the appropriate blank. (If students do not have copies of the sample paper, they can write on separate sheets of paper.)

4. Ask students to compare their responses with those of a partner. They should take a few minutes to talk about the paper and ask each other questions. Expect this process to be slow at first; they will talk more and come to agreement faster as time goes on.

Discussing the Paper

Discuss the paper with the class. Ask students to say what scores they gave the paper and why. The *why* is the most important part in deepening their understanding. Use the following questions to encourage discussion:

• Can you picture students doing their best to irritate the teacher?

• What is the writer's main idea? Express it in your own words.

• Can you see this as a scene in a movie? Who would play the teacher?

• Do the details suggest that this writer has thoroughly examined the topic (annoying the teacher)? Do you think the writer could have told us more?

*Rationale for the Score**

Most students should see this paper as fairly **strong.** It received a score of **4,** based on the 6-point rubric. It has a clear main idea: It's easy to drive your teacher crazy. The writer also includes details in the form of suggestions: students might make annoying noises, interrupt, and so on. It is easy to picture what the writer is talking about, though more precise details would help provide a more vivid experience. We do not actually hear the teacher speak—or hear the students' responses. Also, the dog-that-eats-the-homework story is a bit of a cliché. Still, the student has fun with this light story and encourages readers to have fun, too.

Extensions

1. Ask each student to look at a piece of his or her own writing. Is the main idea clear? If not, what can be done to make it clear? Are the details interesting? Will additional changes help?

2. Start with a general statement, such as *The teacher went crazy.* Ask students to give you details to flesh out the picture and turn it into something vivid. Try to do it without using the word *crazy.* (Hint: Show what the teacher does. Have him or her speak.)

3. Ask student pairs to revise "How to Drive Your Teacher Crazy." Encourage them to think through the issue prior to writing. Ask for volunteers to read their "before" and "after" versions.

*See Teacher's Guide page 194 for a 5-point rubric and page 206 for the score.

Sample Paper 1: IDEAS

How to Drive Your Teacher Crazy

It's not really hard as it sounds. Driving your teacher **really** crazy, that is. All you really need to know is what drives you or your parents crazy! You should know. They hate when you interrupt them in the middle of a conversation or when they are talking on the phone. You know what? A teacher could get even more annoyed.

To drive a teacher super crazy, interrupt a lot, until she's ready to blow. When she's at the point, stop. After about five minutes, make slurping noises, burp, or make any other annoying or disgusting noises nobody can stand. When she turns around or starts to yell, tell her you can't help it if you have to burp, or that slurping's a habit you can't seem to get rid of. What teachers hate more than anything is excuses.

Ever wonder why you end up doing homework when you don't really want to? It's because you know your teacher will blow up if you tell her your dog ate your homework. Especially if you do not even have a dog.

There you go. All the tips on annoying your teacher and what to watch out for. Just remember to bring your ear plugs. . . .

Mark the score that this paper should receive in the trait of IDEAS.
Read your rubric for Ideas to help you decide.

___1 ___2 ___3 ___4 ___5 ___6___

Sample Paper 2: Boomer

Objective

Students will learn how interesting details and a strong main idea make writing clear and easy to understand.

Materials

Student Rubric for Ideas (Teacher's Guide page 5)

Sample Paper 2: Boomer (Teacher's Guide page 125 and/or Transparency 2)

Scoring the Paper

1. Give each student a copy of the sample paper and the Student Rubric for Ideas. Use the rubric to focus students' attention on the key features of the trait of IDEAS—a strong main idea and details that support it. The main idea should be clear and the details strong enough to create a picture in the reader's mind.

2. Have students think about these questions as they listen to you read the paper: *Is the main idea clear? Are the details strong?*

3. Ask students to score the paper *individually,* using the rubric. They should mark their scores in writing, putting an **X** in the appropriate blank. (If students do not have copies of the sample paper, they can write on separate sheets of paper.)

4. Ask students to compare their responses with those of a partner. They should take a few minutes to talk about the paper and ask each other questions. Expect this process to be slow at first; they will talk more and come to agreement faster as time goes on.

Discussing the Paper

Discuss the paper with the class. Ask students to say what scores they gave the paper and why. The *why* is the most important part in deepening their understanding. Use the following questions to encourage discussion:

- Can you picture what is happening in this paper?
- What parts do you picture most clearly?
- What is the writer's main idea? Is it easy to tell?
- Does this writer select interesting details to share about Boomer? What are some examples?

*Rationale for the Score**

Most students should see this paper as **strong.** It received a score of **6,** based on the 6-point rubric. The writer paints a clear, vivid picture of what it is like to have a new puppy in the house. The story shows how caring for a new pet is not as simple as people sometimes think it will be. Notice that the writer goes beyond generalities to include specific details, such as Boomer's bumping into things, chewing on everything in sight, and staining the living room rug.

Extensions

1. Ask each student to look at a piece of his or her own writing. Ask students to write **G** in the margin for "generality" and **S** for "specific detail." Then, have them see how many **G**'s they can turn into **S**'s.

2. Ask students to write a story about a pet—their own or someone else's. The story could revolve around a good or not-so-good experience or (as with *Boomer*) a combination of the two.

3. Using the information the writer provides as a starting point, write about Boomer's introduction to the family from Mom's, Dad's, or Boomer's point of view.

4. First-time pet owners often have some unexpected experiences. A brochure could be helpful. Invite students to create a brochure that could be distributed to a first-time buyer of a puppy, a kitten, a fish, or any other pet and who might need an insider's help to manage the situation.

* See Teacher's Guide page 194 for a 5-point rubric and page 206 for the score.

name: .... date: ....

Sample Paper 2: IDEAS

Boomer

I thought I'd be 40 years old before I would get my first dog, but one day my Mom picked me up from school and whisked me off to a farm where golden retriever puppies were for sale. We left with a great puppy that we named Boomer

From day one, he just boomed through the house. Boom! Into the couch. Boom! Into the cupboards. Boom! Into the bedroom door. We loved Boomer so much, but it wasn't easy. He chewed on everything, including my dad's watchband, the newspaper, table mats, rugs, and lamp cords.

Puppies leave other messes, too, and Boomer was no exception. He didn't get the part about going outside before "messing up," as Mom called it, so I had some unpleasant work to do cleaning the kitchen floor, the bathroom floor, and the living room rug! It took a month before Boomer was trained, and by then, we needed new carpeting.

Puppies are cute, cuddly, and sometimes a pain, but I wouldn't trade Boomer for the whole world now. If I had known how much trouble he would be, though, I would have thought twice before bringing him home.

Mark the score that this paper should receive in the trait of IDEAS.
Read your rubric for Ideas to help you decide.

___ 1 ___ 2 ___ 3 ___ 4 ___ 5 ___ 6

Sample Paper 3: Dolly

Objective

Students will understand the importance of developing a main idea and using specific details to support and clarify that main idea.

Materials

Student Rubric for Ideas (Teacher's Guide page 5)

Sample Paper 3: Dolly (Teacher's Guide page 128 and/or Transparency 3)

Scoring the Paper

1. Give each student a copy of the sample paper and the Student Rubric for Ideas. Use the rubric to focus students' attention on the key features of the trait of IDEAS—a strong main idea and details that support it. Review that the details should be specific and relate to the main idea.

2. Have students think about these questions as they listen to you read the paper: *What is the main idea? Are the details specific enough to answer all your questions?*

3. Ask students to score the paper *individually,* using the rubric. They should mark their scores in writing, putting an **X** in the appropriate blank. (If students do not have copies of the sample paper, they can write on separate sheets of paper.)

4. Ask students to compare their responses with those of a partner. They should take a few minutes to talk about the paper and ask each other questions. Expect this process to be slow at first; they will talk more and come to agreement faster as time goes on.

5. After three or four minutes, ask students to write their reasons for scoring the paper as they did.

Discussing the Paper

Discuss the paper with the class. Ask students to say what scores they gave the paper and why. The *why* is the most important part in deepening their understanding. Use the following questions to encourage discussion:

- What is this writer's main idea? Is it easy to identify?
- Does the writer choose good details to help make the main idea clear?
- Are you, as a reader, left with any questions about Dolly or Aunt Beth? If so, what questions?
- Is there any unneeded information in the paper?

*Rationale for the Score**

Most students should see this paper as **in process.** It received a score of **3,** based on the 6-point rubric, because more information is needed to make this paper complete. The main idea could be that Hawaii is an interesting place, or it could be that swimming with dolphins is exciting. Most of the details relate to the first topic, but the title seems to suggest that the writer meant to tell something about Dolly. The writer needs to choose a definite topic and stick with it. In addition, most of the paper is filled with generalities about Hawaii: It is green, it is beautiful, you can swim or walk on the beach, and so on. These are things most readers know already. It would be interesting to learn more about swimming with dolphins. What is that like? Did Aunt Beth have fun? What skills does it take to swim with dolphins?

Extensions

1. Ask each student to look at a piece of his or her own writing. Is the main idea clear? Does it match the title of the paper? If not, ask students to brainstorm possible new titles that will not mislead readers.

2. Ask students to do some research on swimming with dolphins. How did this activity get started? Do people still do it? What experiences have they had? See whether, as a class, you can come up with four or five interesting bits of information that would add spice to this story.

3. Ask students to imagine they are the owners or operators of a business that invites tourists to swim with dolphins. What might an advertisement for such a business look like? Have students create posters, brochures, or newspaper ads for this business.

* See Teacher's Guide page 194 for a 5-point rubric and page 206 for the score.

Sample Paper 3: IDEAS

Dolly

This year my family took a vacation to Hawaii. In case you do not know, Hawaii is a long chain of islands in the Pacific Ocean. They are very green and beautiful. There is a lot to do in Hawaii, such as shopping or swimming or taking pictures of the beautiful scenery. Or you can just walk on the beach and watch the sunset. It is so beautiful! While we were in Hawaii, my Aunt Beth went swimming with the dolphins. One of the dolphins was named Dolly. She was very friendly. We have a picture of them together, and it is so cool. I still have it. You should take a vacation in Hawaii if you get the chance. You will not forget it!

Mark the score that this paper should receive in the trait of IDEAS. Read your rubric for Ideas to help you decide. Then write your reason for the score.

___ 1 ___ 2 ___ 3 ___ 4 ___ 5 ___ 6

_____

_____

Compare your score with your partner's. How did you do?

____ We matched **exactly!**

____ We matched within **one point**—pretty good!

____ We were **two points or more** apart. We need to discuss this.

Sample Paper 4: Least Favorite Chore

Objective

Students will learn that a writer needs to focus on a topic and use details to support that topic.

Materials

Student Rubric for Ideas (Teacher's Guide page 5)

Sample Paper 4: Least Favorite Chore (Teacher's Guide page 131 and/or Transparency 4)

Scoring the Paper

1. Give each student a copy of the sample paper and the Student Rubric for Ideas. Use the rubric to focus students' attention on the key features of the trait of IDEAS—a strong main idea and details that support it. Review that the main idea should be clear and easy to identify.

2. Have students think about these questions as they listen to you read the paper: *Does the writer focus on the topic? Is the title appropriate?*

3. Ask students to score the paper *individually,* using the rubric. They should mark their scores in writing, putting an **X** in the appropriate blank. (If students do not have copies of the sample paper, they can write on separate sheets of paper.)

4. Ask students to compare their responses with those of a partner. They should take a few minutes to talk about the paper and ask each other questions. Expect this process to be slow at first; they will talk more and come to agreement faster as time goes on.

5. After three or four minutes, ask students to write the reasons for scoring the paper as they did.

Discussing the Paper

Discuss the paper with the class. Ask students to say what scores they gave the paper and why. The *why* is the most important part in deepening their understanding. Use the following questions to encourage discussion:

• Does this writer provide a clear picture of his or her least favorite chore?

• What does the writer spend the most time talking about? Is this the main idea?

• Do you still have questions, or does the writer provide enough information?

• Could any information be left out without hurting the paper? If so, what?

*Rationale for the Score**

Most students should see this paper as **weak.** It received a score of **2,** based on the 6-point rubric, because it lacks focus and switches topics too much. The title provides a clue to the topic; the writer apparently intends to write about his or her least favorite chore but never does (The least favorite seems to be washing dishes, yet cleaning his or her room isn't high on the list either.) The paper quickly loses focus and moves on to describe the brothers' chores and how the writer wishes to have their jobs. This writer needs to pick a topic and then select details that support the topic. We do not know, for example, why the writer hates doing dishes so much except that it is messy and takes a long time.

Extensions

1. Ask each student to look at a piece of his or her own writing. Is the main idea clear? If not, what can be done to make it clear? Are the details interesting? Will additions or changes help?

2. Brainstorm a list of chores many people do not like. Have each student choose one and write a paper about it. It could be a story (a time when . . .) or perhaps a persuasive piece (why this chore isn't as bad as the reader might think).

3. Hold a debate. Have students debate which chore is the worst (or most educational or most helpful) and explain why. Ask the class to evaluate who presents the most convincing evidence.

4. Have the class rate "Least Favorite Chore" for voice. Is the voice score higher than the score for ideas? Why? Would improving the ideas increase the voice score even more? Why or why not?

*See Teacher's Guide page 194 for a 5-point rubric and page 207 for the score.

Sample Paper 4: IDEAS
Least Favorite Chore

I have to do a lot of chores around the house. My brothers do, too, but I think mine is the worst. Washing dishes is messy and takes forever. We all have to clean our rooms, too. The worst part is figuring out which clothes are the dirty ones and then hanging the other ones up. After you do the laundry, you cannot tell whose socks are whose. My brother Brad gets the best chore, which is vacuuming. That takes about five minutes and you get to vacuum up stuff other people dropped! This is a fabulous way of tormenting your brother when he is getting on your nerves. Bill feeds the cat. Big deal. Like that takes a lot of talent. He usually forgets to do that, and I end up doing it for him. I think when you do other people's chores you should get their allowance. And then the other thing is you should rotate so you do not have to do the same chore every week.

Mark the score that this paper should receive in the trait of IDEAS. Read your rubric for Ideas to help you decide. Then write your reason for the score.

___ 1 ___ 2 ___ 3 ___ 4 ___ 5 ___ 6

_____

_____

Compare your score with your partner's. How did you do?

___ We matched **exactly!**

___ We matched within **one point**—pretty good!

___ We were **two points or more** apart. We need to discuss this.

Organization

Sample Paper 5: How to Snowboard

Objective

Students will learn that a paper can have strong moments in one trait even though it is not consistently strong in that trait.

Materials

Student Rubric for Organization (Teacher's Guide page 23)

Sample Paper 5: How to Snowboard (Teacher's Guide page 134 and/or Transparency 5)

Scoring the Paper

1. Give each student a copy of the sample paper and the Student Rubric for Organization. Use the rubric to focus students' attention on the key features of the trait of ORGANIZATION—a strong lead, a strong conclusion, and details that are carefully connected.

2. Have students think about these questions as they listen to you read aloud the paper: *Does one idea flow smoothly to the next? Do you like the beginning and ending?*

3. Ask students to score the paper *individually,* using the rubric. They should mark their scores in writing, putting an **X** in the appropriate blank. (If students do not have copies of the sample paper, they can write on separate sheets of paper.)

4. Ask students to compare their responses with those of a partner. They should take a few minutes to talk about the paper and ask each other questions. Expect this process to be slow at first; they will talk more and come to agreement faster as time goes on.

5. After three or four minutes, ask students to write the reasons for scoring the paper as they did.

Discussing the Paper

Discuss the paper with the class. Ask students to say what scores they gave the paper and why. The *why* is the most important part in deepening their understanding. Use the following questions to encourage discussion:

• Do you like the way the writer begins the paper (the lead)? Why?

• Do you like the way the writer ends it (the conclusion)? Why?

• Are ideas and details carefully connected (by strong transitions)? Can you point to a place that is strong or weak?

• Does the writer ever wander from the main topic? If so, where?

*Rationale for the Score**

Most students should see this paper as fairly **strong.** It received a score of **4,** based on the 6-point rubric, because it is easy to follow and has a reasonably good lead and conclusion. The main problem is that the writer moves from one detail to another very rapidly. For example, we never find out what a *superman* is—or a *double black diamond.* This may be common jargon among snowboarders, but the paper is obviously written for a beginner. (See the first line.) Better transitions also would have helped build a picture of what skills snowboarders truly need.

Extensions

1. Ask each student to look at a piece of his or her own writing. Are the key points and details in order? If not, how can the paper be revised by moving things around? Is there a strong lead and conclusion? Have students write new conclusions as needed. Also ask them to look for recognizable organizational patterns. Can they describe these patterns in their own words?

2. Have students write three other leads the writer might use for this paper. Have them do the same with the conclusions.

3. Score "How to Snowboard" for the trait of ideas. Chances are, your score will be lower than for organization. Talk about why this might happen.

*See Teacher's Guide page 195 for a 5-point rubric and page 207 for the score.

Sample Paper 5: ORGANIZATION

How to Snowboard

You want to learn to snowboard? Well, it's not as easy as it looks! The very first thing to do is get fitted with a snowboard, boots, and bindings. Then, you have to find out if you are a "Goofy" or a "Regular" rider. You find this out by standing straight then having someone push you back. The foot you fall back on is the foot you put to the back when snowboarding. Most people are "Regulars"—left foot forward. I, on the other hand, am a "Goofy"—right foot forward. Next, you need to take lessons so you don't do a superman off a jump and take a gallon of snow in your face. One good thing to remember is this: Always know how and when to stop, and NEVER try to do a double black diamond on your first day. Be careful on the chair lifts. Another thing, practice makes perfect. Happy riding!

Mark the score that this paper should receive in the trait of ORGANIZATION. Read your rubric for Organization to help you decide. Then write your reason for the score.

_____ 1 _____ 2 _____ 3 _____ 4 _____ 5 _____ 6

_____

_____

Compare your score with your partner's. How did you do?

_____ We matched **exactly!**

_____ We matched within **one point**—pretty good!

_____ We were **two points or more** apart. We need to discuss this.

Sample Paper 6: A Day to Remember

Objective

Students will recognize that even when a writer tells things as he or she remembers them, the writing can seem disorderly if the writer cannot make a connection to a larger idea.

Materials

Student Rubric for Organization (Teacher's Guide page 23)

Sample Paper 6: A Day to Remember (Teacher's Guide page 137 and/or Transparency 6)

Scoring the Paper

1. Give each student a copy of the sample paper and the Student Rubric for Organization. Use the rubric to focus students' attention on the key features of the trait of ORGANIZATION—a strong lead, a strong conclusion, and details that are carefully connected.

2. Have students think about this question as they listen to you read aloud the paper: *Does the paper have a strong organization, one that is easy to follow?*

3. Ask students to score the paper *individually,* using the rubric. They should mark their scores in writing, putting an **X** in the appropriate blank. (If students do not have copies of the sample paper, they can write on scratch paper.) Suggest that students mark the text by putting an X next to places where the writer seems to wander from the main topic.

4. Then, ask students to compare their responses with those of a partner. They should take a few minutes to talk about the paper and ask each other questions. Expect this process to be slow at first; they will talk more and come to agreement faster as time goes on.

5. After three or four minutes, ask students to write the reasons for scoring the paper as they did.

Discussing the Paper

Discuss the paper with the class. Ask students to say what scores they gave the paper and why. The *why* is the most important part in deepening their understanding. Use the following questions to encourage discussion.

- Does this paper have a strong beginning (lead)? Why do you think so?
- Does it have a strong conclusion? Why do you think so?
- Is it easy to follow? Does the writer stick to one main point or jot down thoughts as they pop into his or her head? Can you give an example of a place where the thoughts do not seem to connect?

Rationale for the Score*

Most students should see this paper as **weak.** It received a score of **1,** based on the 6-point rubric, because it is a collection of random thoughts with no main point. There is no real lead; the paper just begins. There is no conclusion, either; the paper simply stops when the writer runs out of things to say. It would be very difficult to identify an organizational pattern since almost nothing connects to anything else. It could be argued that these are all "events the writer remembers." Still, the details are too general to give the piece any clear focus or sense of purpose.

Extensions

1. Ask each student to look at a piece of his or her own writing and revise it to make stronger connections between details and to create more complete leads and conclusions.

2. The notion of "A Day to Remember" is vague. Have students think of a more specific title and then read the piece again as a class to see which details connect everything to this main idea.

*See Teacher's Guide page 195 for a 5-point rubric and page 208 for the score.

Sample Paper 6: ORGANIZATION

A Day to Remember

So when we got to the barbecue, a lot of people were already eating. I was not that hungry, so I played croquet with some kids I did not know. They were not that good, and I won. We stayed for awhile. We drank lemonade, and mine had a lot of seeds in it! There was a dog that kept stealing food from everyone's plate. I forget his name. Then the next day we all went sailing on this humongous boat. You could swim off the boat and climb back up a ladder on the side. My dad caught a fish. What I remember most is my outrageous sunburn. I couldn't sleep for most of the first night.

Mark the score that this paper should receive in the trait of ORGANIZATION. Read your rubric for Organization to help you decide. Then write your reason for the score.

—— 1 —— 2 —— 3 —— 4 —— 5 —— 6

_____

_____

Compare your score with your partner's. How did you do?

—— We matched **exactly!**

—— We matched within **one point**—pretty good!

—— We were **two points or more** apart. We need to discuss this.

Sample Paper 7: Grizzly Bears

Students will understand that a clear organizational pattern with a strong lead and a strong conclusion makes writing interesting and easy to follow.

Materials

Student Rubric for Organization (Teacher's Guide page 23)

Sample Paper 7: Grizzly Bears (Teacher's Guide page 140 and/or Transparency 7)

Scoring the Paper

1. Give each student a copy of the sample paper and the Student Rubric for Organization. Use the rubric to focus students' attention on the key features of the trait of ORGANIZATION—a strong lead, a strong conclusion, and details that are carefully connected.

2. Have students think about these questions as they listen to you read aloud the paper: *Is the paper easy to follow? Is there a particular pattern you can follow?*

3. Ask students to score the paper *individually,* using the rubric. They should mark their scores in writing, putting an **X** in the appropriate blank. (If students do not have copies of the sample paper, they can write on separate sheets of paper.)

4. Ask students to compare their responses with those of a partner. They should take a few minutes to talk about the paper and ask each other questions. Expect this process to be slow at first; they will talk more and come to agreement faster as time goes on.

Discussing the Paper

Discuss the paper with the class. Ask students to say what scores they gave the paper and why. The *why* is the most important part in deepening their understanding. Use the following questions to encourage discussion:

- Was this paper easy to follow? Can you recall most of the information this writer shared about grizzly bears? Why do you think that is?

- Do you like the way the writer begins the paper (the lead)? Why? Would you change it?

- Do you like the way the writer ends the paper (the conclusion)? Why? Would you change it?

- Does the writer do a good job of linking details to the main idea?

*Rationale for the Score**

Most students should see this paper as very **strong.** It received a score of **6,** based on the 6-point rubric, because it is easy to follow and understand. The writer makes an important point at the beginning: There may be some surprises about grizzlies. The writer does a good job of linking details and facts to this main idea. The lead and conclusion are both strong. The writer starts by telling the reader to expect a few surprises and ends by predicting the future for grizzly bears—they won't be a problem much longer since they won't be around much longer.

Extensions

1. Ask each student to look at a piece of his or her own writing and describe the organizational pattern. Is there any recognizable pattern? Should there be? (Possible patterns: step-by-step, comparison-contrast, order of events, most important to least important, and so on.)

2. Problem-solution is a good organizational pattern to use when writing. Give students a chance to try this pattern by proposing a solution to the problem of the dwindling grizzly bear population. Is the problem serious or exaggerated? Should anything be done? If so, what? (Some research will, of course, result in stronger papers!)

*See Teacher's Guide page 195 for a 5-point rubric and page 208 for the score.

Sample Paper 7: ORGANIZATION

Grizzly Bears

You probably think you know a lot about grizzly bears, but you might be surprised by certain facts. For example, maybe you did not know that there were once over 50,000 grizzly bears in the American West—and that does not even count the state of Alaska, where many grizzlies still live today. That huge number has dwindled to a pathetic 1,000 grizzlies outside of Alaska.

One enemy of the grizzly bear is the trophy hunter. It is no longer legal to hunt grizzlies, but they can be shot legally if they attack someone or pose a danger to human life. However, we are the main enemy. A full-grown grizzly needs 400 square miles of wilderness in which to hunt, find food and shelter, and raise cubs. That wilderness land is getting harder to find and that is because of people. Each year we build more roads, put up more houses and commercial buildings, and encroach further into the wilderness, leaving the animals with nowhere to go. We should stop. Chances are, though, that we won't. Many people value civilization much more than they value wildlife. It won't be a problem for grizzlies much longer, though. They probably won't be here.

Mark the score that this paper should receive in the trait of ORGANIZATION. Read your rubric for Organization to help you decide.

___ 1 ___ 2 ___ 3 ___ 4 ___ 5 ___ 6

Sample Paper 8: Getting Stitches

Objective

Students will recognize the importance of presenting events in logical order and of relating the lead and the conclusion to the rest of the paper.

Materials

Student Rubric for Organization (Teacher's Guide page 23)

Sample Paper 8: Getting Stitches (Teacher's Guide page 143 and/or Transparency 8)

Scoring the Paper

1. Give each student a copy of the sample paper and the Student Rubric for Organization. Use the rubric to focus students' attention on the key features of the trait of ORGANIZATION—a strong lead, strong conclusion, and details that are carefully connected.

2. Have students think about these questions as they listen to you read aloud the paper: *Is the paper easy to follow? Is there a particular pattern you can follow?*

3. Ask students to score the paper *individually*, using the rubric. They should mark their scores in writing, putting an **X** in the appropriate blank. (If students do not have copies of the sample paper, they can write on separate sheets of paper.)

4. Ask students to compare their responses with those of a partner. They should take a few minutes to talk about the paper and ask each other questions. Expect this process to be slow at first; they will talk more and come to agreement faster as time goes on.

5. After three or four minutes, ask students to write the reasons for scoring the paper as they did.

Discussing the Paper

Discuss the paper with the class. Ask students to say what scores they gave the paper and why. The *why* is the most important part in deepening their understanding. Use the following questions to encourage discussion.

- Do you like the lead? Why? Does the rest of the paper follow from the lead?
- Is this paper easy to follow?
- Do you see any pattern in the organizational structure? If so, can you describe it?
- Does the conclusion work? Why?
- What would you do differently to make this paper stronger in organization?

*Rationale for the Score**

Most students should see this paper as **weak.** It received a score of **2,** based on the 6-point rubric, because it wanders randomly and leaves to the reader the task of putting the story together. The information is there; it's just presented in a confusing order that is hard to follow. The lead works fairly well: *Having stitches is no fun.* The writer seems to have a definite story in mind: getting stitches. But he or she is easily distracted. Furthermore, the reader is bounced from point to point, from the stitches, to Todd, then to the accident, then to the experience in the hospital, and then back to the fall. There is no real conclusion. The paper just stops.

Extensions

1. Ask each student to review a piece of writing he or she is working on. Is any information out of place? If so—how can things be put in order? Have students draw a line through any information that is unneeded? Ask volunteers to share versions 1 and 2. You may even wish to make overheads of students' work so they can show their editing or revision to the class.

2. Have each student write a brief note to the writer of "Getting Stitches," offering advice on strong organization.

3. Have students score "Getting Stitches" for the trait of IDEAS. Is the score higher or lower than for organization? Have students explain why they think this is.

* See Teacher's Guide page 195 for a 5-point rubric and page 208 for the score.

Sample Paper 8: ORGANIZATION

Getting Stitches

Having stitches is no fun. None of this would have happened if I had not tried to climb a rope into the tree house. We built the tree house last summer, and Todd had this really bright idea of being able to get into it using only a rope. Todd has been my friend since first grade, and he is the only person I share my secrets with. So we were going to put knots in the rope so you would have something to hang on to or put your feet on. That was the idea. But I was in a hurry to try it out, and the next thing I knew I slipped. I went to Mercy Hospital, and I had to wait a really long time for the nurse to look at me. When you have stitches, they give you something to kill the pain, but it does not kill it entirely. When I fell, I hit my head on a log or rock or something. I got a huge cut in my forehead, and that is where I had to have the stitches.

Mark the score that this paper should receive in the trait of ORGANIZATION. Read your rubric for Organization to help you decide. Then write your reason for the score.

___ 1 ___ 2 ___ 3 ___ 4 ___ 5 ___ 6

_____

_____

Compare your score with your partner's. How did you do?

____ We matched **exactly!**

____ We matched within **one point**—pretty good!

____ We were **two points or more** apart. We need to discuss this.

Sample Paper 9: Lose the Hiccups

Objective

Students will learn how strong voice can make writing lively and entertaining.

Materials

Student Rubric for Voice (Teacher's Guide page 41)

Sample Paper 9: Lose the Hiccups (Teacher's Guide page 146 and/or Transparency 9)

Scoring the Paper

1. Give each student a copy of the sample paper and the Student Rubric for Voice. Use the rubric to focus students' attention on the key features of the trait of VOICE—high energy, vivid impressions, a sense of the author's interest in and passion for the topic.

2. Have students think about these questions as they listen to you read the paper: *Would you want to read this aloud? What part has especially strong voice?*

3. Ask students to score the paper *individually,* using the rubric. They should mark their scores in writing, putting an **X** in the appropriate blank. (If students do not have copies of the sample paper, they can write on separate sheets of paper.)

4. Ask students to compare their responses with those of a partner. They should take a few minutes to talk about the paper and ask each other questions. Expect this process to be slow at first; they will talk more and come to agreement faster as time goes on.

Discussing the Paper

Discuss the paper with the class. Ask students to say what scores they gave the paper and why. The *why* is the most important part in deepening their understanding. Use the following questions to encourage discussion:

- Did you enjoy listening to this story? Did you want to hear more? Why?

- Would you read this aloud to a friend? Why?

- Does this writer seem to enjoy telling this story? What clues do we have about how the writer feels?

- Are there particular words or images that contribute to the voice? Which ones?

*Rationale for the Score**

Most students should see this paper as **strong.** It received a score of **6,** based on the 6-point rubric, because the voice is lively and engaging. The writer creates vivid impressions of her annoyance at being unable to concentrate during the math test, her grandmother's strategies, and the "final strategy" that takes the hiccups away. The writer seems to enjoy telling the story and invites readers to laugh along with her. The writer's voice never loses that high energy level. We can picture everything that happens, and the humorous images add to the fun.

Extensions

1. Ask a volunteer to read aloud "Lose the Hiccups." Tell students to listen but not to follow along. Do they *hear* the voice? Discuss whether it is easy to read with expression.

2. Ask students to identify those passages in "Lose the Hiccups" in which the voice is strongest. Talk about specific passages that contribute to the voice.

3. Ask students, in groups or pairs, to read their own writing aloud. They should listen for moments of voice in one another's writing and comment on those parts they think are strongest. Participate as a writer/reader in one of the groups.

* See Teacher's Guide page 196 for a 5-point rubric and page 209 for the score.

Sample Paper 9: VOICE

Lose the Hiccups

"Hush up! I mean it!" I said to my friend Stephanie. We were taking a math test, and I didn't want to blow it. But every time I thought I had an answer, she would let out this hysterical, high-pitched hiccup, and I would lose my whole train of thought. Somehow, I struggled through the math test; then I confronted her in the hall. "OK," I said, taking her by the hand, "Come with me."

Now, my grandmother had several surefire cures for hiccups, but none of them were too practical. One was to drink hot lemonade. It's gross, but it works for some people. It's hard to cook it in school, though. Another was to hold a toad next to your neck. I wasn't about to ask Stephanie to try that one! So, I was forced into the final strategy. I waited until Stephanie was nice and relaxed, getting something out of her locker and, of course, hiccuping away as if this were as normal as breathing. Then POW! I leaped at her, making my worst witch face and shrieking at the top of my lungs. She was terrified and dropped everything from her arms. I was afraid she would throw up and then we'd have a new thing to cure. But—the hiccups stopped. Now, maybe it was fear, or maybe it was her being so mad at me. I'm not sure. She isn't speaking to me right now, but I sure am doing a lot better on my tests!

Mark the score that this paper should receive in the trait of VOICE.
Read your rubric for Voice to help you decide.

—— 1 —— 2 —— 3 —— 4 —— 5 —— 6

Sample Paper 10: Climbing Rocket Butte

Objective

Students will understand that a paper can have strong moments even if it is not consistently strong.

Materials

Student Rubric for Voice (Teacher's Guide page 41)

Sample Paper 10: Climbing Rocket Butte (Teacher's Guide page 149 and/or Transparency 10)

Scoring the Paper

1. Give each student a copy of the sample paper and the Student Rubric for Voice. Use the rubric to focus students' attention on the key features of the trait of VOICE—high energy, vivid impressions, and a sense of the author's interest in and passion for the topic.

2. Have students think about these questions as they listen to you read the paper: *Did you enjoy listening to this paper read aloud? How does the writer feel about the climb?*

3. Ask students to score the paper *individually,* using the rubric. They should mark their scores in writing, putting an **X** in the appropriate blank. (If students do not have copies of the sample paper, they can write on separate sheets of paper.)

4. Ask students to compare their responses with those of a partner. They should take a few minutes to talk about the paper and ask each other questions. Expect this process to be slow at first; they will talk more and come to agreement faster as time goes on.

Discussing the Paper

Discuss the paper with the class. Ask students to say what scores they gave the paper and why. The *why* is the most important part in deepening their understanding. Use the following questions to encourage discussion:

- Can you tell how the writer feels about climbing? Which clues show you?

- Are some moments stronger than others? Where are they?

- Would you read this aloud to a friend? Why?

- Does this writer seem to enjoy writing about climbing Rocket Butte?

- If you read another piece of writing by this same author, do you think you would recognize the voice? Why?

Rationale for the Score*

Most students should see this paper as **in process.** It received a score of **3,** based on the 6-point rubric. The voice is not especially passionate, but it is not disinterested, either. What the reader misses is the insight into this writer's true feelings. Does the writer resent the fact that Ben races ahead? We suspect he does, but he doesn't really show it. How much do his feet hurt? How thirsty is he really? How rough is the terrain? Is the view at the top worth it? Many questions remain. Readers want to see, hear, and feel what's happening in this writer's world. More details, an insider's perspective, and lively language would make the voice stronger—this paper reads much the way the writer apparently felt while climbing Rocket Butte.

Extensions

1. Ask student pairs to revise "Climbing Rocket Butte" for the trait of VOICE. They may add, delete, or change any details they wish. Ask them first to imagine all the things that might have made this climb less than enjoyable. Then tell them to revise the paper, writing from that point of view so that strong feelings come through. Read revisions aloud.

2. Suggest that each student review any piece of writing on which he or she is currently working to identify strong *moments* of voice. The next step is to see whether the paper can be revised to give it even more of those strong moments.

3. Have students create a class poster called *Tips for Strong Voice.* Tell them to include on the poster as many tips for creating strong voice as possible.

* See the Teacher's Guide page 196 for a 5-point rubric and page 209 for the score.

Sample Paper 10: VOICE

Climbing Rocket Butte

Climbing Rocket Butte was the hardest thing I have ever done. At least it is the hardest thing I can remember! It all happened on a Saturday. My dad, my brother Ben, and I were all going to do the climb. We got up early and got our pass for the butte. It was about two miles to the top. First, we drove to the trailhead, where we had to show our passes. We parked the car in a good spot. Then, it was time to start the climb. We had all brought water bottles, and I made sure to wear my good hiking shoes that do not hurt my feet. Ben, who is a good climber, had to show off from the very beginning. He practically ran up the first hill. After that, I didn't see too much of him because he was so far ahead of me on the trail. Dad stayed with me, but he wanted to go ahead I could tell. He didn't, though. At first, it was kind of nice having company, but after a while, I felt too tired to talk so I didn't care that much. I had to stop and take a drink or catch my breath every few yards, it seemed. It was hard work climbing that butte. It took me a couple of hours, and of course Ben was already at the top waving when I got there. I don't know how long it took him, but not that long. I might go again, but it wouldn't be my first choice of things to do on a Saturday.

Mark the score that this paper should receive in the trait of VOICE.
Read your rubric for Voice to help you decide.

____ 1 ____ 2 ____ 3 ____ 4 ____ 5 ____ 6

Sample Paper 11: Parking the Car with Dad

Objective

Students will learn how energy, individuality, and situational detail contribute to strong voice.

Materials

Student Rubric for Voice (Teacher's Guide page 41)

Sample Paper 11: Parking the Car with Dad (Teacher's Guide page 152 and/or Transparency 11)

Scoring the Paper

1. Give each student a copy of the sample paper and the Student Rubric for Voice. Use the rubric to focus students' attention on the key features of the trait of VOICE—high energy, vivid impressions, and a sense of the author's interest in and passion for the topic.

2. Have students think about these questions as they listen to you read the paper: *Does the writer show an interest in the subject? Which parts have strong voice?*

3. Ask students to score the paper *individually*, using the rubric. They should mark their scores in writing, putting an **X** in the appropriate blank. (If students do not have copies of the sample paper, they can write on separate sheets of paper.)

4. Ask students to compare their responses with those of a partner. They should take a few minutes to talk about the paper and ask each other questions. Expect this process to be slow at first; they will talk more and come to agreement faster as time goes on.

Discussing the Paper

Discuss the paper with the class. Ask students to say what scores they gave the paper and why. The *why* is the most important part in deepening their understanding. Use the following questions to encourage discussion:

- Do you think you might recognize this writer's voice in another piece of writing? Why?

- Were there any moments of strong voice you could identify?

- How would you describe this writer's voice?

- Can you think of anything that would make the voice even stronger? If so, what?

- Do you think the writer is interested in this topic? What clues tell you how the writer feels?

*Rationale for the Score**

Most students should see this paper as **strong.** It received a score of **5,** based on the 6-point rubric. The voice is full of energy and highly individual. The writer creates a portrait of her father. This paper can be seen as a character sketch, and we learn a lot about Dad: He is fussy, he's a fanatic about his car, he doesn't mind a little inconvenience if the car won't be damaged, and he assumes others (for example, Mom) will agree with his way of doing things. The specific details that describe what Dad does, or does not do, help the reader picture him, which is what gives the paper strong voice.

Extensions

1. Tell students to create character sketches using this writer's technique; ask them to place the character in a situation in which he or she will display "typical" behavior. Show the character being cranky, fussy, shy, outspoken, or whatever. Share results aloud.

2. Ask students to create dialogues between the Dad and Mom characters as they are portrayed in "Parking the Car with Dad." You might set up the situation: Mom is driving for a change and parks in a place Dad does not approve of. What conversation might they have?

3. Do your students agree that the first few lines do not have quite as much voice as the rest of the paper? If so, see whether they can come up with a new lead that projects as much voice as the paper in general. You may wish to have them work in pairs on this.

* See the Teacher's Guide page 196 for a 5-point rubric and page 209 for the score.

Sample Paper 11: VOICE

Parking the Car with Dad

People have their own ways of doing things. My dad is no exception. He has his own way of parking the car, and it's pretty different from my mom's. I'm sure he assumes Mom drives just the way he does. Ha! Mom drives into a parking lot and takes the first space she finds that is closest to the door. This is, I think, the way most people park. Well, not my dad. First, he sizes up the lot—which spots will be hard to back out of, where might he run into a delivery truck, that kind of thing. He avoids those spots, naturally. Then, he looks for shade. Shade is a big plus. However, he won't go for shade if it means giving up safety. See, my dad has this thing about getting the car dinged. He does not like to park close to other drivers or near posts or anything he might hit his door on when getting in and out. He also avoids curbs because they might damage the tires. Parking near the door is the least of my dad's concerns. "You don't mind a little walk, do you?" is his motto. And I don't. Only we park so far away just to avoid other cars, I sometimes wonder why we didn't just walk from home in the first place. Some days, Dad has trouble finding the right spot. Then we have to move several times. When we finally get home, Mom always says, "What took you so long?"

Mark the score that this paper should receive in the trait of VOICE.
Read your rubric for Voice to help you decide.

___ 1 ___ 2 ___ 3 ___ 4 ___ 5 ___ 6

Sample Paper 12: Too Much Television

Objective

Students will understand that a paper can have little or no voice if the writer seems bored or does not put much of himself or herself into the writing.

Materials

Student Rubric for Voice (Teacher's Guide page 41)

Sample Paper 12: Too Much Television (Teacher's Guide page 155 and/or Transparency 12)

Scoring the Paper

1. Give each student a copy of the sample paper and the Student Rubric for Voice. Use the rubric to focus students' attention on the key features of the trait of VOICE— high energy, vivid impressions, and a sense of the author's interest in and passion for the topic.

2. Have students think about these questions as they listen to you read the paper: *Does the writer sound engaged or bored? How can you tell?*

3. Ask students to score the paper *individually,* using the rubric. They should mark their scores in writing, putting an **X** in the appropriate blank. (If students do not have copies of the sample paper, they can write on separate sheets of paper.)

4. Ask students to compare their responses with those of a partner. They should take a few minutes to talk about the paper and ask each other questions. Expect this process to be slow at first; they will talk more and come to agreement faster as time goes on.

5. After three or four minutes, ask students to write the reasons for scoring the paper as they did.

Discussing the Paper

Discuss the paper with the class. Ask students to say what scores they gave the paper and why. The *why* is the most important part in deepening their understanding. Use the following questions to encourage discussion:

- Would you want this story to go on for several more pages? Why or why not?
- Would you want to read another piece by this same writer? Why or why not?
- Does this writer seem to enjoy telling this story? What clues do we have about how the writer feels?
- What word(s) would you use to describe this writer's voice?

*Rationale for the Score**

Most students should see this paper as **weak.** It received a score of **1,** based on the 6-point rubric. It has little or no voice; it is basically a recitation of observations. The writer sounds tired—and less than excited about this topic. The writer seems to have nothing to say and seems to be filling space so that the chore of writing about television can be finished. As a result, the paper is a collection of generalities with virtually no personal insights or observations. It is not individual. It does not seem likely that many students would choose to share the piece aloud. How does this writer *really* feel about watching TV? Is he sharing the real scoop?

Extensions

1. Suppose a friend comes over to watch TV with the writer. Ask students to create dialogue that shows what might happen between the two characters.

2. What if this writer did a review of a TV show—any show at all. Have students describe what the review might be about? You may also wish to ask students to do a personal review of the same show. How do the reviews compare?

3. Invite students to write a response to this paper. Is television as dismal a form of entertainment and information as this writer makes it out to be? Or is there another way of viewing this topic? Read responses aloud, and invite students to listen for and comment on strong moments of voice.

* See the Teacher's Guide page 196 for a 5-point rubric and page 210 for the score.

Too Much Television

How much television do you watch? It might not be that good for you. If you watch news, that could be a good thing. You learn things about our world. We need to know what is happening in the world. We also need to learn the weather so we are ready for what tomorrow brings. Some shows are not that useful. A lot of comedies do not show real life. They might make you laugh, but they are not the way life really is. Some shows might make you depressed or make you bored. The other thing is that if you are watching TV, you are not doing other things like exercising or studying. A lot of people do not get work done because of television. They also do not exercise and could gain weight. So watch some TV, but not too much, and you will be happy.

Mark the score that this paper should receive in the trait of VOICE. Read your rubric for Voice to help you decide. Then write your reason for the score.

——— 1 ——— 2 ——— 3 ——— 4 ——— 5 ——— 6

_____

_____

Compare your score with your partner's. How did you do?

——— We matched **exactly!**

——— We matched within **one point**—pretty good!

——— We were **two points or more** apart. We need to discuss this.

Sample Paper 13: Pasta, Pasta, Pasta!

Objective

Students will recognize that clear, simple languages can create vivid impressions.

Materials

Student Rubric for Word Choice (Teacher's Guide page 41)

Sample Paper 13: Pasta, Pasta, Pasta! (Teacher's Guide page 158 and/or Transparency 13)

Scoring the Paper

1. Give each student a copy of the sample paper and the Student Rubric for Word Choice. Use the rubric to focus students' attention on the key features of the trait of WORD CHOICE—strong verbs and sensory words (words that show how things look, sound, smell, taste, and feel). Vague or overused words weaken the writing.

2. Have students think about this question as they listen to you read the paper: *Which words paint a clear picture in your mind?*

3. Ask students to score the paper *individually,* using the rubric. They should mark their scores in writing, putting an **X** in the appropriate blank. (If students do not have copies of the sample paper, they can write on separate sheets of paper.)

4. Ask students to compare their responses with those of a partner. They should take a few minutes to talk about the paper and ask each other questions.

5. After three or four minutes, ask students to write the reasons for scoring the paper as they did.

Discussing the Paper

Discuss the paper with the class. Ask students to say what scores they gave the paper and why. The *why* is the most important part in deepening their understanding. Use the following questions to encourage discussion:

• Do you have favorite words or phrases in this paper? Which ones?

• Are there any words you think could or should be replaced? Which ones?

• Could you make a movie out of this paper? Why?

• Can you tell how the writer feels? Which words show you?

Rationale for the Score*

Most students should see this paper as fairly **strong.** It received a score of **5,** based on the 6-point rubric. Though the paper still could use revision, it does have examples of good word choice. Some students may argue that the verbs could be a little stronger. This paper could also benefit from more sensory detail because it focuses on food. At the same time, the writer tells enough and tells it clearly enough that it is very easy to picture this family at dinner.

Extensions

1. Ask students to revise "Pasta, Pasta, Pasta!," by adding a few strong verbs and one or two sensory details that might enrich the picture. Read revisions aloud to see whether the improvements are significant.

2. Invite students to write about a food experience of their own. They might have eaten something new or something they did not care for, or perhaps they cooked something that did not turn out the way they expected. Remind them to include strong verbs and sensory details to bring the paragraph to life. Share results aloud.

3. Have each student look at a piece of his or her own writing and underline any words that are weak or overused. Ask each student to then brainstorm—alone or with a partner—some better word choices. Discuss the difference this revision makes for the overall sound of the paper.

*See Teacher's Guide page 197 for a 5-point rubric and page 210 for the score.

Sample Paper 13: WORD CHOICE

Pasta, Pasta, Pasta!

My sister is learning to cook, and she is not that bad at it, either. The thing is, she is totally hung up on pasta. It seems like it is the only thing we eat. We have spaghetti one night, lasagna the next, tortellini the next . . . well, you get the idea. Don't get me wrong. I like pasta. At least I used to. My mom tells me to be patient. Let her get really good at this and then she will move on to something else. I say she is good enough now. I mean, how much can you ruin pasta? (Well, our school cafeteria can, but they overcook everything.) Here's another thing. Sheri (my sister) always thinks she is cooking for a dozen people. So she makes this huge mound of, say, spaghetti. Then we eat till we're bursting, and it doesn't even make a dent in the amount she made. Mom says, "Oh, good—we'll have some leftovers!" This is when my stomach does a flip-flop. knowing that I have to eat pasta every day for a week is too much. Next week is my birthday, and when I blow out my candles on my manicotti cake, I think you can guess what I will be wishing for.

Mark the score that this paper should receive in the trait of WORD CHOICE. Read your rubric for Word Choice to help you decide. Then write the reason for your score.

___ 1 ___ 2 ___ 3 ___ 4 ___ 5 ___ 6

_____

_____

Sample Paper 14: Autumn—My Favorite Season!

Objective

Students will learn that overuse of sensory detail can weaken writing rather than strengthen it.

Materials

Student Rubric for Word Choice (Teacher's Guide page 41)

Sample Paper 14: Autumn—My Favorite Season (Teacher's Guide page 161 and/or Transparency 14)

Scoring the Paper

1. Give each student a copy of the sample paper and the Student Rubric for Word Choice. Use the rubric to focus students' attention on the key features of the trait of WORD CHOICE— strong verbs and sensory words (words that show how things look, sound, smell, taste, and feel). Overuse of particular words weaken the writing.

2. Have students think about these questions as they listen to you read the paper: *Which words stand out as strong? Are there any overused words?*

3. Ask students to score the paper *individually,* using the rubric. They should mark their scores in writing, putting an **X** in the appropriate blank. (If students do not have copies of the sample paper, they can write on separate sheets of paper.)

4. Ask students to compare their responses with those of a partner. They should take a few minutes to talk about the paper and ask each other questions.

5. After three or four minutes, ask students to write the reasons for scoring the paper as they did.

Discussing the Paper

Discuss the paper with the class. Ask students to say what scores they gave the paper and why. The *why* is the most important part in deepening their understanding. Use the following questions to encourage discussion:

- Which words in this paper did you find most lively and interesting?

- Do you notice any strong verbs? Name them.

- Are any words overused? Which ones?

- Can you picture what this writer is describing? What helps you picture it? Does anything make it difficult to bring the picture into focus?

*Rationale for the Score**

Most students should see this paper as **in process.** It received a **3,** based on the 6-point rubric, even though it has some real strengths, such as the use of strong verbs: *crunching, caresses, stroll* (although *stroll* does not go with *briskly*), *fluff,* and so on. This writer also tries very hard to use sensory detail to create a rich picture of the autumn landscape. The problem is *too much* detail, and the result is overwhelming. This writer needs to pull back and focus on a few significant sensory details. Some students may wish to give this paper a 5 or 6, thinking, "The more, the better." In good writing, though, simplicity can be a virtue.

Extensions

1. Work with students to identify some phrases that may be overdone in "Autumn—My Favorite Season." Simplify these phrases and then read the resulting paragraph aloud. Is simpler better? Can sensory language be overdone?

2. Ideally, students should use sensory language—not overuse it. Ask each student to examine a piece of his or her own writing, looking for examples of sensory language. Students should underline passages and then ask themselves, "Do I have enough sensory information to make the paper interesting? Do I have too much, so readers will feel overwhelmed?" Then have them revise accordingly.

3. Ask students to score "Autumn—My Favorite Season!" for voice. Chances are that the score will not be as high as students might have predicted. Discuss the relationship between word choice and voice. Can too much information slow a reader down? Does this affect voice?

*See Teacher's Guide page 197 for a 5-point rubric and page 210 for the score.

Sample Paper 14: WORD CHOICE

Autumn—My Favorite Season!

Crunching through the crispy leaves, my eyes gaze at the wondrous blue of the shimmering sky with the fluffy clouds sailing across it like little boats and the sounds of chirping birds filling the crispy air with the ringing of their bright, cheerful songs. The snappy, crispy air caresses my face with its frosty fingers as I briskly stroll through the colorful leaves and twigs surrounding my meandering path. Cool breezes fluff my hair as I look across the glimmering glow of the ever-changing forest with its leaves rustling softly in the wind. I smell the smoldering warmth of fall fires and the simmering goodness of homemade soup warming on the hot stove. Autumn is my favorite time of year.

Mark the score that this paper should receive in the trait of WORD CHOICE. Read your rubric for Word Choice to help you decide. Then write the reason for your score.

___ 1 ___ 2 ___ 3 ___ 4 ___ 5 ___ 6

_____

_____

Compare your score with your partner's. How did you do?

___ We matched **exactly!**

___ We matched within **one point**—pretty good!

___ We were **two points or more** apart. We need to discuss this.

Sample Paper 15: Desert Creatures

Objective

Students will learn how clear, original word choice enhances writing.

Materials

Student Rubric for Word Choice (Teacher's Guide page 41)

Sample Paper 15: Desert Creatures (Teacher's Guide page 164 and/or Transparency 15)

Scoring the Paper

1. Give each student a copy of the sample paper and the Student Rubric for Word Choice. Use the rubric to focus students' attention on the key features of the trait of WORD CHOICE— strong verbs and sensory words (words that show how things look, sound, smell, taste, and feel). Vague or overused words weaken the writing.

2. Have students think about these questions as they listen to you read the paper: *Would you want to read this aloud? Are any words overused or repeated?*

3. Ask students to score the paper *individually,* using the rubric. They should mark their scores in writing, putting an **X** in the appropriate blank. (If students do not have copies of the sample paper, they can write on separate sheets of paper.)

4. Ask students to compare their responses with those of a partner. They should take a few minutes to talk about the paper and ask each other questions.

5. After three or four minutes, ask students to write the reasons for scoring the paper as they did.

Discussing the Paper

Discuss the paper with the class. Ask students to say what scores they gave the paper and why. The *why* is the most important part in deepening their understanding. Use the following questions to encourage discussion:

- Do you notice any strong verbs? Name them.
- Are any words new to you? If so, can you tell the meaning from the way the writer uses them?
- Does this writer use vague words or clichés? Is the writing fairly original?
- Do the words paint a clear picture in your mind? Why?

*Rationale for the Score**

Most students should see this paper as very **strong.** It received a **6,** based on the 6-point rubric, because the word choice is striking and original: *earth's creatures, found ingenious ways, invades the desert, courtesy of nature, extracting water from what it eats,* and so on. The paper is virtually free of overused words, jargon, or clichés, and though the vocabulary is strong, it is not overdone. This is writing to inform—not to impress. It is quite easy to determine meaning from context. Consider especially the way the writer uses the words *listless, ingenious, transported, extracting, arid, adaptable,* and *instinct.* Striking word choice, including strong word choice, makes this paper an excellent example of how to use words well.

Extensions

1. Discuss any words from this paper that were new to your students. Make a list. Then, talk about whether the writer makes meaning clear from context.

2. As a class, underline or circle favorite words and phrases. Then, ask students to look at writing they are currently working on and do the same. Are there any words or phrases they would like to change?

3. Invite students to use words and phrases from "Desert Creatures" to create a poem about the desert. Students can work in pairs. Be sure to read results aloud.

*See Teacher's Guide page 197 for a 5-point rubric and page 211 for the score.

Sample Paper 15: Word Choice

Desert Creatures

If you've ever felt weak and thirsty on a hot day, you may have wondered how animals manage to survive and find water in the heat of a desert. Actually, some have found ingenious ways of adapting.

Although not everyone knows this, drinkable water often arrives in the desert in the form of early morning fog. Desert beetles take advantage of this precious water supply, rising early to let droplets of dew form on their bodies. Presto! A refreshing drink—and it is delivered daily, courtesy of nature.

Over thousands of years, animals have learned to seek out stored water from plants, such as cactus and even tiny seeds. The kangaroo rat is so clever at extracting water from what it eats that it rarely has to drink pure water at all!

People are adaptable, too, of course. We wear light clothing, sunscreen, and big hats to keep out the heat. We've invented fans and air conditioning. Plus, we dig wells and irrigate even in arid regions. But face it: We have technology to help us. Animals have adapted very well, and they've done it all without special tools or equipment.

Mark the score that this paper should receive in the trait of WORD CHOICE. Read your rubric for Word Choice to help you decide.

_____ 1 _____ 2 _____ 3 _____ 4 _____ 5 _____ 6

Sample Paper 16: Something I Learned to Do

Objective

Students will learn that vague, imprecise language can create an unclear picture in the reader's mind.

Materials

Student Rubric for Word Choice (Teacher's Guide page 41)

Sample Paper 16: Something I Learned to Do (Teacher's Guide page 167 and/or Transparency 16)

Scoring the Paper

1. Give each student a copy of the sample paper and the Student Rubric for Word Choice. Use the rubric to focus students' attention on the key features of the trait of WORD CHOICE— strong verbs and sensory words (words that show how things look, sound, smell, taste, and feel). Words that are misused or unclear from the context weaken the writing.

2. Have students think about this question as they listen to you read the paper: *Are words used clearly and correctly?*

3. Ask students to score the paper *individually,* using the rubric. They should mark their scores in writing, putting an **X** in the appropriate blank. (If students do not have copies of the sample paper, they can write on separate sheets of paper.)

4. Ask students to compare their responses with those of a partner. They should take a few minutes to talk about the paper and ask each other questions.

Discussing the Paper

Discuss the paper with the class. Ask students to say what scores they gave the paper and why. The *why* is the most important part in deepening their understanding. Use the following questions to encourage discussion:

- Were any words unclear? Which ones?

- Were any words repeated too often? Which ones?

- Are there any words this writer should explain that are not explained? Which ones?

- Do you get a clear picture of what this writer is talking about? Why?

*Rationale for the Score**

Most students should see this paper as **weak.** It received a **2,** based on the 6-point rubric. It is possible to figure out what the "something I learned to do" is—framing a picture—but this is not clear at the beginning. Unclear language hides the message and makes the steps of picture framing difficult to visualize. The writer certainly overuses some words: *fun, part, things, stuff.* In addition, these words are too vague. The paper finally springs to life in the last line; more of this voice and stronger word choice is needed throughout.

Extensions

1. Make a list of words from "Something I Learned to Do" that should not be used if a writer wants his or her message to be clear. Then ask students, in teams, to rewrite the paper, avoiding these words. Read the results aloud.

2. Ask whether anyone in your class has had this writer's experience of framing a picture. If so, invite this person to do an oral critique: Are important points or steps left out? What else should this writer have told us? Are things explained correctly?

3. Ask students to imagine that they are proprietors of a frame shop where people can frame their own art. Invite them to create posters or flyers advertising the frame shop. Make sure students give the shop a name, specify the services the shop provides, and choose strong words to describe the shop.

*See Teacher's Guide page 197 for a 5-point rubric and page 211 for the score.

Sample Paper 16: WORD CHOICE

Something I Learned to Do

This is the most fun thing I have ever learned to do! First, you pick out your frame and then the part that goes inside, the mat. You can choose your own colors, which is the really fun part. I had a hard time deciding because I liked so many different ones. The frame and the other parts have to be cut to fit. This means measuring things out so you get things just right. It is not that hard, but measuring is the hardest part because if you do not measure right, things do not fit, and you might even have to start over. Some parts of your picture, like the corners, will be held together with nails and for some things you need glue. This is the part I thought was the most fun, but as I said, if you don't do it right, everything could turn out crooked! Put the mat on, and hold it down while you fit the frame on a piece at a time. Later, you will have some kind of paper on the back, but you don't need to worry about that for right now. The people at the frame shop might help you with this part because it is kind of hard. They will also help you mount the hooks or wire if you use wire. There! You're done! Now hang your picture on the wall proudly, and enjoy a piece of art you made yourself!

Mark the score that this paper should receive in the trait of WORD CHOICE. Read your rubric for Word Choice to help you decide.

_____ 1 _____ 2 _____ 3 _____ 4 _____ 5 _____ 6

Sample Paper 17: Dinosaurs in the Movies

Objective

Students will recognize that rambling and run-on sentences have a negative impact on sentence fluency.

Materials

Student Rubric for Sentence Fluency (Teacher's Guide page 77)

Sample Paper 17: Dinosaurs in the Movies (Teacher's Guide page 170 and/or Transparency 17)

Scoring the Paper

1. Give each student a copy of the sample paper and the Student Rubric for Sentence Fluency. Use the rubric to focus students' attention on the key features of the trait of SENTENCE FLUENCY—a variety of sentence beginnings and sentence lengths, no run-ons or rambling sentences, and a generally smooth flow that's easy on the ear.

2. Have students think about this question as they listen to you read the paper: *Do you hear any rambling sentences (sentences with too many connecting words like* and *or* but)?

3. Ask students to score the paper *individually,* using the rubric. They should mark their scores in writing, putting an **X** in the appropriate blank. (If students do not have copies of the sample paper, they can write on separate sheets of paper.)

4. Ask students to compare their responses with those of a partner. They should take a few minutes to talk about the paper and ask each other questions.

5. After three or four minutes, ask students to write the reasons for scoring the paper as they did.

© Great Source. Copying is prohibited.

Discussing the Paper

Discuss the paper with the class. Ask students to say what scores they gave the paper and why. The *why* is the most important part in deepening their understanding. Use the following questions to encourage discussion:

- Did you notice any rambling sentences—sentences that go on and on with lots of connecting words? Did they help or hurt the fluency?

- Did you notice any run-on sentences? Did they help or hurt the fluency?

- Is it hard to read this paper aloud? Do you need to practice? Why? (Be sure students have a chance to try reading this paper aloud before answering.)

*Rationale for the Score**

Most students should see this paper as **weak.** It received a **2,** based on the 6-point rubric, because the sentences are long, rambling, and repetitive. This makes the writer sound breathless! It is difficult to make this paper sound smooth without some rehearsal. With some sentence reconstruction and attention to varied beginnings, this could be a very strong paper. The writer has used some imagination, but the paragraph needs revision.

Extensions

1. Invite volunteers to read aloud "Dinosaurs in the Movies." Let several students try. Discuss the difficulties of reading this paper aloud.

2. Ask students to practice reading pieces of their own writing aloud. What sentence fluency problems do they encounter? This is a good time for some revision!

3. "Dinosaurs in the Movies" is a good paper to revise in two-person teams. Remind students to look for sentences that are punctuated incorrectly and sentences that are long and rambling. When students finish, invite teams to read their revisions aloud and compare them with the original. Also invite team members to identify the specific problems they found and the strategies they used to solve them.

*See Teacher's Guide page 198 for a 5-point rubric and page 211 for the score.

Sample Paper 17: SENTENCE FLUENCY

Dinosaurs in the Movies

I read quite a lot about dinosaurs and I know quite a lot about them from books and magazines and also I have an uncle who is a paleontologist which if you don't know is a scientist who studies fossils and ancient life forms. The point I am trying to make is that dinosaurs the way they do them in the movies because first of all they are robots and you can tell by the way they move they aren't real. But like when they are after people and biting off their heads or trying to eat them and stuff that is not very realistic because dinosaurs **mostly** were vegetarian except for T-rex and a couple others, and besides they spent huge amounts of time just grazing or sleeping or hanging out in the swamps and not chasing everything in sight. But Hollywood is just trying to get people to the movies so they do this by trying to scare you to death only when something is fake it isn't all that scary anyhow if you ask me it's mostly just annoying. I don't go to many dinosaur movies and that's why. My uncle doesn't go to any!

Mark the score that this paper should receive in the trait of SENTENCE FLUENCY. Read your rubric for Sentence Fluency to help you decide. Then write your reason for the score.

___ 1 ___ 2 ___ 3 ___ 4 ___ 5 ___ 6

_____

_____

_____

Sample Paper 18: Sneezing Etiquette

Objective

Students will recognize how well-crafted, varied sentences create a smooth, fluent paper.

Materials

Student Rubric for Sentence Fluency (Teacher's Guide page 77)

Sample Paper 18: Sneezing Etiquette (Teacher's Guide page 173 and/or Transparency 18)

Scoring the Paper

1. Give each student a copy of the sample paper and the Student Rubric for Sentence Fluency. Use the rubric to focus students' attention on the key features of the trait of SENTENCE FLUENCY—a variety of sentence beginnings and sentence lengths, no run-ons or rambling sentences, and a generally smooth flow that's easy on the ear.

2. Have students think about these questions as they listen to you read the paper: *How does the paper sound? Does it read smoothly? Does the dialogue sound natural?*

3. Ask students to score the paper *individually,* using the rubric. They should mark their scores in writing, putting an **X** in the appropriate blank. (If students do not have copies of the sample paper, they can write on separate sheets of paper.)

4. Ask students to compare their responses with those of a partner. They should take a few minutes to talk about the paper and ask each other questions.

Discussing the Paper

Discuss the paper with the class. Ask students to say what scores they gave the paper and why. The *why* is the most important part in deepening their understanding. Use the following questions to encourage discussion:

• Did you think the paper sounded smooth when you heard it read aloud? Were any parts choppy? Do you think you could read it aloud without difficulty?

• As you looked and listened to this paper, what did you notice about the sentence beginnings? Did this help or hurt the fluency?

• Notice the dialogue. Do you think it sounds natural? Why?

*Rationale for the Score**

Most students should see this paper as very **strong.** It received a **6,** based on the 6-point rubric, because it exhibits virtually all of the qualities necessary for fluent writing. It is easy to read with expression, and oral reading helps bring out the fluency. Nearly every sentence begins differently; the variety is great. In addition, sentences vary in length, so the writing is never monotonous. The dialogue is not extensive, but what is there has a very natural sound and contributes to the voice.

Extensions

1. Invite students to read "Sneezing Etiquette" aloud. Is it easy to read? If you have scored and discussed "Dinosaurs in the Movies," compare the two for sentence fluency. They are very different—but what makes the difference?

2. Invite students to score this paper for the trait of VOICE. Chances are the score, will be high. Discuss the connection between fluency and voice. Why are more fluent papers also likely to be stronger in voice?

3. Ask students to create a dialogue between the writer and one of the sneezers he describes—or between two or more sneezers, if you prefer. First, ask students to come up with situations. Perhaps the two people are at the movies, in a restaurant, or in an elevator. Have some fun with this one, and read the results aloud. Try writing a dialogue yourself, and share it with your students.

*See Teacher's Guide page 198 for a 5-point rubric and page 212 for the score.

Sample Paper 18: SENTENCE FLUENCY
Sneezing Etiquette

What really bothers me is how some people sneeze. I know what you're thinking: "People can't really help sneezing." That's true—to a point. Everyone sneezes now and then, especially if a person has allergies or uses too much pepper. However, there are some inexcusable ways to sneeze.

First there is the siren-blast sneeze. This comes from a person who sneezes with the force of a tornado and gives a kind of rodeo yell while doing it. The sneezer may claim that it cannot be helped. Actually, it must take practice.

Then there is the little-bit-at-a-time sneeze. This comes from the person who is too shy to let it all out on the first sneeze and winds up sneezing uncontrollably eighteen times. Let it out, I say! This same person will keep pleading, "Excuse me! Oh, excuse me again! Oh, I'm so sorry!"

What we need is a guide to sneezing etiquette. Always carry tissues, and use them. Step back and turn away if you feel a sneeze coming on. Give one good sneeze instead of a series of tiny sneezes. Kill the scream. Excuse yourself only once. Maybe we can't stop sneezing, but we can do it with good manners.

Mark the score that this paper should receive in the trait of SENTENCE FLUENCY. Read your rubric for Sentence Fluency to help you decide.

____ 1 ____ 2 ____ 3 ____ 4 ____ 5 ____ 6

Sample Paper 19: Seals

Objective

Students will recognize how little variety in sentence structure and sentence length can decrease fluency in a piece of writing.

Materials

Student Rubric for Sentence Fluency (Teacher's Guide page 77)

Sample Paper 19: Seals (Teacher's Guide page 176 and/or Transparency 19)

Scoring the Paper

1. Give each student a copy of the sample paper and the Student Rubric for Sentence Fluency. Use the rubric to focus students' attention on the key features of the trait of SENTENCE FLUENCY—varied sentence beginnings and lengths, no run-ons or rambling sentences, and a generally smooth flow that's easy on the ear.

2. Have students think about these questions as they listen to you read the paper: *Are the sentence beginnings varied? Do the sentences vary in length?*

3. Ask students to score the paper *individually,* using the rubric. They should mark their scores in writing, putting an **X** in the appropriate blank. (If students do not have copies of the sample paper, they can write on separate sheets of paper.)

4. Ask students to compare their responses with those of a partner. They should take a few minutes to talk about the paper and ask each other questions.

5. After three or four minutes, ask students to write the reasons for scoring the paper as they did.

Discussing the Paper

Discuss the paper with the class. Ask students to say what scores they gave the paper and why. The *why* is the most important part in deepening their understanding. Use the following questions to encourage discussion:

- As you looked and listened to this paper, what did you notice about the sentence beginnings? Did this help or hurt the fluency?

- Did you think the paper sounded smooth when you heard it read aloud?

- Do you think reading this paper aloud would be easy or hard? Why do you think so? (Give students time to try this with a partner.)

- Are the sentences varied in length? A little bit? A lot? Does this help or hurt the fluency?

*Rationale for the Score**

Most students should see this paper as **in process.** It received a **3,** based on the 6-point rubric, because there is very little variety in sentence beginnings or sentence length. Most sentences start with the words *They* or *Seals.* The writing is not really difficult to follow, but it is choppy because the sentences are all about the same length. It's hard to give this piece a smooth reading. (Some students may even see it as a **2.**)

Extensions

1. Ask students to try reading "Seals" aloud. Ask two or three different students to read it, and have the rest of the class close their eyes and just listen. What do they hear? Is it fluent?

2. Have students read pieces of their own writing to one another in response groups. They should listen just for the fluency. Remind them to really tune in to sentence beginnings and sentence lengths. Also, they should not hear any run-ons or rambling sentences.

3. "Seals" is a piece that cries out for sentence combining. Ask student pairs to try this technique as a way of putting more fluency into the piece. As students work, they should also take care to begin sentences in different ways. Read results aloud. Be sure to share your own revision as well.

*See Teacher's Guide page 198 for a 5-point rubric and page 212 for the score.

Sample Paper 19: SENTENCE FLUENCY

Seals

Seals are fascinating creatures. Seals are mammals, but they live in the water and spend a lot of time underwater. They need to come up to breathe. Seals have very smooth fur. They can move through the water very rapidly because of this. They are often hunted for their beautiful fur.

Seals are found in oceans all over the world. They can also live in freshwater lakes. This is unusual, though. Mother seals have one baby a year. They are called pups. Seal mothers and pups can get lost in the crowd when big groups of seals live together. They find each other by sound and smell.

Seals that live in the Arctic are usually white when they are pups. This protects them. They cannot be seen against the snow. They turn brown as they grow older.

Some seals are disappearing from the earth. They have been hunted so much that only a few remain. Let's hope people will try to help the seals in the future. Seals are amazing animals!

Mark the score that this paper should receive in the trait
of SENTENCE FLUENCY. Read your rubric for Sentence Fluency
to help you decide. Then write your reason for the score.

____ 1 ____ 2 ____ 3 ____ 4 ____ 5 ____ 6

_____

_____

Sample Paper 20: Birthday Gift

Objective

Students will learn how a natural, conversational style of dialogue contributes to fluency.

Materials

Student Rubric for Sentence Fluency (Teacher's Guide page 77)

Sample Paper 20: Birthday Gift (Teacher's Guide page 179 and/or Transparency 20)

Scoring the Paper

1. Give each student a copy of the sample paper and the Student Rubric for Sentence Fluency. Use the rubric to focus students' attention on the key features of the trait of SENTENCE FLUENCY—a variety of sentence beginnings and sentence lengths, no run-ons or rambling sentences, and a generally smooth flow that's easy on the ear.

2. Have students think about this question as they listen to you read the paper: *Does the dialogue sound natural?*

3. Ask students to score the paper *individually,* using the rubric. They should mark their scores in writing, putting an **X** in the appropriate blank. (If students do not have copies of the sample paper, they can write on separate sheets of paper.)

4. Ask students to compare their responses with those of a partner. They should take a few minutes to talk about the paper and ask each other questions.

Discussing the Paper

Discuss the paper with the class. Ask students to say what scores they gave the paper and why. The *why* is the most important part in deepening their understanding. Use the following questions to encourage discussion:

• Did this paper sound smooth when you heard it read aloud?

• Does the dialogue sound like real conversation?

• Did many sentences in this paper begin differently? What effect did this have on the fluency?

• What would you do to improve the fluency of this paper?

*Rationale for the Score**

Most students should see this paper as **strong.** It received a **5,** based on the 6-point rubric, because the dialogue is strong. The writer and her mom have a real conversation. It sounds natural, and it also advances the story. They have a predicament—what to buy for the writer's picky friend Heather. As they decide on a gift for Heather, we learn something about the writer and her mom. Mom may be a little old-fashioned, but she's also imaginative and a good sport. She has a sense of humor, too. Sentences show a lot of variety—and the piece is easy to read aloud with expression.

Extensions

1. First, invite students to read the piece aloud. You may wish to do this as a reader's theater, with one student reading the part of the writer (give her a name if you wish), one reading the part of the mom, and another reading the part of the narrator.

2. Create an extended dialogue between the writer and her mom—or the writer and Heather. Invite students to begin by setting up the situation. Perhaps it's after the party, discussing what happened, or after the ski lesson, or after the first day on the slopes. Read the results aloud. Talk about dialogue as a technique for developing character.

3. Brainstorm three words to describe Mom, three words to describe Heather, and three words to describe the writer. How do you know what these people are like? How does dialogue influence idea development?

*See Teacher's Guide page 198 for a 5-point rubric and page 212 for the score.

Sample Paper 20: Sentence Fluency

Birthday Gift

"Why don't you just get her something to wear?" my mom said to me. I knew she was trying to be helpful, but I was trying to come up with the perfect gift for my friend Heather, who is the world's pickiest person.

"The right clothes are too hard to find," I told my Mom.

"Well, then, how about a cookbook?" Mom asked me.

"Am I hearing things? You **can't** be serious. That is so weird."

"Well, how about a bottle of water, then?" Mom suggested, only this time I knew she was joking. She had more suggestions up her sleeve, though . . . "A plant? A pet fish? A movie? Wait!" Her face lit up like neon. "I've got it!"

Three days later I was watching Heather unwrap her gift, a card good for one free skiing lesson. Heather squealed with delight when she saw what it was. I knew immediately that she was picturing herself on the slopes. She will have to buy the gear for herself. Maybe my mom is smarter than I thought.

Mark the score that this paper should receive in the trait of SENTENCE FLUENCY. Read your rubric for Sentence Fluency to help you decide.

—— 1 —— 2 —— 3 —— 4 —— 5 —— 6

Sample Paper 21: Kites

Objective

Students will understand that writing strong in conventions helps readers' comprehension.

Materials

Student Rubric for Conventions (Teacher's Guide page 95)

Sample Paper 21: Kites (Teacher's Guide page 182 and/or Transparency 21)

Scoring the Paper

1. Give each student a copy of the sample paper and the Student Rubric for Conventions. Use the rubric to focus students' attention on the key features of the trait of CONVENTIONS—correct spelling, punctuation, grammar, use of capital letters, and use of paragraphs. Be alert for repeated or missing words as well.

2. Have students think about these questions as they read the paper: *Are there many errors in this paper? Do they affect your understanding of what the author is trying to say?*

3. Ask students to score the paper *individually,* using the rubric. They should mark their scores in writing, putting an **X** in the appropriate blank. (If students do not have copies of the sample paper, they can write on separate sheets of paper.)

4. Ask students to compare their responses with those of a partner. They should take a few minutes to talk about the paper and ask each other questions.

5. After three or four minutes, ask students to write the reasons for scoring the paper as they did.

Discussing the Paper

Discuss the paper with the class. Ask students to say what scores they gave the paper and why. The *why* is the most important part in deepening their understanding. Use the following questions to encourage discussion:

- As you read through this paper, did you notice many errors? A few errors? Almost no errors?

- Do the mistakes this writer made slow you down as a reader at all? Where?

- Could the writer get this piece published as is? Why?

*Rationale for the Score**

Most students should see this paper as quite **strong.** It received a **5,** based on the 6-point rubric, because it needs only the lightest editing. There are no errors serious enough to slow a reader down. Some raters may object to the use of multiple exclamation points. This is a stylistic choice, really, and should not lower the score. This writer has done an excellent job of handling conventions effectively and making the text easy to read.

Extensions

1. This text does contain six minor errors. See how many errors your eagle-eye editors can identify—and correct. You will want to use Transparency 21 for this.

2. Take time to identify some of the things this writer does correctly. See how long a list your student editors can come up with.

3. Invite each student to look at a piece of his or her own work and circle the errors. Students can go back and correct their papers later, during another session.

4. Did students identify any "errors" in this piece that were not really errors? (Did they think something had been done incorrectly?) Be sure to take time to discuss these, using examples as necessary.

*See Teacher's Guide page 199 for a 5-point rubric and page 213 for the score.

Sample Paper 21: CONVENTIONS

Kites

I love kites. Every time I go to the beach I have to get a new new kite. My parents won't pay for this luxury, so I have save my own allowance and babysitting money to make it happen. My favorites are the dragon kites with huge tails that billow in the wind. They are amazing. When I get a kite up without having it crash into the sand, I think I must be experiencing that same feeling a pilot gets flying a plane into the sky. There's a moment when you think you've let out too much string and its going to get away from you. Then the wind catches it just right and theres a bit of lift—and wow! Your soaring!!

Mark the score that this paper should receive in the trait of CONVENTIONS. Read your rubric for Conventions to help you decide. Then write your reason for the score.

____ 1 ____ 2 ____ 3 ____ 4 ____ 5 ____ 6

_____

_____

Compare your score with your partner's. How did you do?

____ We matched **exactly!**

____ We matched within **one point**—pretty good!

____ We were **two points or more** apart. We need to discuss this.

Sample Paper 22: Traffic Flow

Objective

Students will recognize that conventional errors, if serious enough, can distract the reader.

Materials

Student Rubric for Conventions (Teacher's Guide page 95)

Sample Paper 22: Traffic Flow (Teacher's Guide page 185 and/or Transparency 22)

Scoring the Paper

1. Give each student a copy of the sample paper and the Student Rubric for Conventions. Use the rubric to focus students' attention on the key features of the trait of CONVENTIONS—correct spelling, punctuation, grammar, use of capital letters, and use of paragraphs. Be alert for repeated or missing words as well.

2. Have students think about these questions as they read the paper: *Are there many errors in this paper? Do they affect your understanding of what the author is trying to say?*

3. Ask students to score the paper *individually,* using the rubric. They should mark their scores in writing, putting an **X** in the appropriate blank. (If students do not have copies of the sample paper, they can write on separate sheets of paper.)

4. Ask students to compare their responses with those of a partner. They should take a few minutes to talk about the paper and ask each other questions.

5. After three or four minutes, ask students to write the reasons for scoring the paper as they did.

Discussing the Paper

Discuss the paper with the class. Ask students to say what scores they gave the paper and why. The *why* is the most important part in deepening their understanding. Use the following questions to encourage discussion:

- As you read through this paper, did you notice many errors? A few errors? Almost no errors?

- Did the mistakes this writer made slow you down at all as a reader? Did they ever get in the way of the writer's message? If so, where?

- How much work would it take to get this paper ready for publication? A lot? A little?

*Rationale for the Score**

Most students should see this paper as **weak.** It received a **2,** based on the 6-point rubric, because it contains enough errors to slow a reader down. Editing this would be quite a task. It will need line-by-line editing to prepare it for publication. It can be argued that of the many errors, several involve the misspelling of the word *traffic.* If the student corrected this one misspelling, it would significantly decrease the number of errors.

Extensions

1. Ask students to count the number of errors they circled in "Traffic Flow." Use a general continuum, on which students vote for one of the following: numerous errors, some errors, a few tiny errors, hardly any errors. Most students should vote for numerous errors. Anyone who finds 15 or more deserves a round of applause.

2. Have students edit "Traffic Flow" individually and then as partners. Not all students will find every error but some might. When you edit together, using Transparency 22, your student editors can help you identify all the errors. Be sure to explain any they do not understand.

*See Teacher's Guide page 199 for a 5-point rubric and page 213 for the score.

Sample Paper 22: CONVENTIONS
Traffic Flow

We have an intersting problem in our town It is a small town and doesnt have that much trafic, but we do not have any trafic lights. Some one came up with the bright idea of having two trafic lights instaled at each end of town now personally I think this would help a lot with the trafic flow. It is almost imposible to make a left turn during "rush hour." Ha ha. I am kidding about that. We do not really have have a rush hour, but if we did have trafic lights it sure would make driving a hole lot easer!

Mark the score that this paper should receive in the trait of CONVENTIONS. Read your rubric for Conventions to help you decide. Then write your reason for the score.

___ 1 ___ 2 ___ 3 ___ 4 ___ 5 ___ 6

_____

_____

Compare your score with your partner's. How did you do?

____ We matched **exactly!**

____ We matched within **one point**—pretty good!

____ We were **two points or more** apart. We need to discuss this.

Sample Paper 23: I Can't Believe It!

Objective

Students will recognize that errors in conventions can interfere with the writer's message.

Materials

Student Rubric for Conventions (Teacher's Guide page 95)

Sample Paper 23: I Can't Believe It! (Teacher's Guide page 188 and/or Transparency 23)

Scoring the Paper

1. Give each student a copy of the sample paper and the Student Rubric for Conventions. Use the rubric to focus students' attention on the key features of the trait of CONVENTIONS—correct spelling, punctuation, grammar, use of capital letters, and use of paragraphs. Be alert for repeated or missing words as well.

2. Have students think about these questions as they read the paper: *Are there many errors in this paper? Do they affect your understanding of what the author is trying to say?*

3. Ask students to score the paper *individually,* using the rubric. They should mark their scores in writing, putting an **X** in the appropriate blank. (If students do not have copies of the sample paper, they can write on separate sheets of paper.)

4. Ask students to compare their responses with those of a partner. They should take a few minutes to talk about the paper and ask each other questions.

5. After three or four minutes, ask students to write the reasons for scoring the paper as they did.

Discussing the Paper

Discuss the paper with the class. Ask students to say what scores they gave the paper and why. The *why* is the most important part in deepening their understanding. Use the following questions to encourage discussion:

- As you read through this paper, did you notice many errors? A few errors? Almost no errors?

- Is there any place in this paper where conventional errors slow you down?

- How much editing will it take to get this paper ready for publication?

- Does this writer have one main problem with conventions (for example, spelling)? Or does she have a variety of problems?

*Rationale for the Score**

Most students should see this paper as **weak.** It received a **1,** based on the 6-point rubric, because even though the paper is quite short, it contains 36 errors. This is more than enough to impair readability. Moreover, there are various kinds of errors in punctuation, spelling, repeated words, unnecessary words, capitalization, and so on. This piece will require word-by-word editing to prepare it for publication.

Extensions

1. Ask students to edit "I Can't Believe It!" so that it would be ready to print in a school newsletter. This is going to be quite a task, so you may wish to have students edit the first half of the paper on one day and the second half on another day.

2. This writer clearly has many difficulties with conventions. Ask students to create a list of teaching strategies that might help a student like this.

3. Using the errors in this paper as models, ask each student to write a conventions quiz: a sentence containing just one conventional error. Students can make their quizzes as tricky as they like! Then, ask each student to exchange his or her sentence with a partner to see whether he or she can find each other's errors. When everyone is finished, share stories. Find out who had the toughest, trickiest error to track down?

4. Score a corrected version of "I Can't Believe It!" for ideas and for voice. The scores should go up! Talk about how weak conventions can hide voice and ideas.

*See Teacher's Guide page 199 for a 5-point rubric and page 213 for the score.

Sample Paper 23: CONVENTIONS

I Can't Believe It!

I can't beleive what my mother did with our living room rug. You woud not believe it either she we had this really neat old brown rug that was just fine yeah it had some ketchup spills from when my litle brother ate their big deal she replaced it with a new carpet that is shartroose. you cant believe this coler do you know what shartroose is even? it is a cross bitween limes and caneries. it is greenish yellow it is uglier than the uglest coler you have ever seen in your lif. it is pretty hard to have freinds over, when you have this funny looking looking rug how do i explain this

Mark the score that this paper should receive in the trait of CONVENTIONS. Read your rubric for Conventions to help you decide. Then write your reason for the score.

_____ 1 _____ 2 _____ 3 _____ 4 _____ 5 _____ 6

_____

_____

Compare your score with your partner's. How did you do?

_____ We matched **exactly!**

_____ We matched within **one point**—pretty good!

_____ We were **two points or more** apart. We need to discuss this.

Sample Paper 24: I Could Swim Forever

Objective

Students will learn how easy reading can be when the writer takes time for careful editing.

Materials

Student Rubric for Conventions (Teacher's Guide page 95)

Sample Paper 24: I Could Swim Forever (Teacher's Guide page 191 and/or Transparency 24)

Scoring the Paper

1. Give each student a copy of the sample paper and the Student Rubric for Conventions. Use the rubric to focus students' attention on the key features of the trait of CONVENTIONS—correct spelling, punctuation, grammar, use of capital letters, and use of paragraphs. Be alert for repeated or missing words as well.

2. Have students think about these questions as they read the paper: *Is this piece of writing ready to be published? Why or why not?*

3. Ask students to score the paper *individually,* using the rubric. They should mark their scores in writing, putting an **X** in the appropriate blank. (If students do not have copies of the sample paper, they can write on separate sheets of paper.)

4. Ask students to compare their responses with those of a partner. They should take a few minutes to talk about the paper and ask each other questions.

5. After three or four minutes, ask students to write the reasons for scoring the paper as they did.

Discussing the Paper

Discuss the paper with the class. Ask students to say what scores they gave the paper and why. The *why* is the most important part in deepening their understanding. Use the following questions to encourage discussion:

- As you read through this paper, did you notice many errors? A few errors? Almost no errors?

- Is there any place in this paper where conventional errors slow you down? If so, where?

- Do you think this paper is ready for publication? Why or why not?

*Rationale for the Score**

Most students should see this paper as very **strong.** It received a **6,** based on the 6-point rubric, because there is only one small error in conventions (a repeated word, *am,* in the second line). This writer uses conventions effectively to make the writing easy to read. The paper does contain fragments, which added to the stylistic effect and are purposeful. Fragments aside, this paper is virtually ready for publication as is—with only one small change. It is important for students to understand that control and skillful use, not perfection, are required for a high score in this trait.

Extensions

1. Create a draft on the overhead on any topic your students select. As you write, slip in some conventional errors. See how quickly students can spot the errors. Under 5 seconds: 5 points. Under 10 seconds: 2 points. Over 10 seconds: You point out the error—no points! The goal is to earn 50 points with no more than 15 errors total.

2. Score "I Could Swim Forever" for other traits—students' choice. Are other scores as strong as the score for conventions? Read the paper aloud, asking students not to follow along. What do they hear? What are the strongest traits, other than conventions? Do any traits need work? Which ones?

*See Teacher's Guide page 199 for a 5-point rubric and page 214 for the score.

Sample Paper 24: CONVENTIONS

I Could Swim Forever

You've heard the expression "Hit the ground running." Well, that's how I hit the pool, only I am swimming, of course. But I am am in motion from the moment my body touches the water. Something about swimming makes me feel more alive than anything else in the world. The chill of the water on my body pushes me on. I love the way I glide through it. Before I know it, I am at the end of the pool, and it is time to turn around. I love the turn, but I always find myself wishing the pool were longer. Eventually, I want to do distance swimming and go for miles. This is who I am. Swimmers have to get up at 4 A.M. to practice. I never mind. I am ready to go long before the alarm sings out. Blow that whistle. Watch me go. You haven't seen the best of me yet. Only dolphins can outswim me.

Mark the score that this paper should receive in the trait of CONVENTIONS. Read your rubric for Conventions to help you decide. Then write your reason for the score.

____ 1 ____ 2 ____ 3 ____ 4 ____ 5 ____ 6

_____

_____

Compare your score with your partner's. How did you do?

____ We matched **exactly!**

____ We matched within **one point**—pretty good!

____ We were **two points or more** apart. We need to discuss this.

Appendix

Using a 5-Point Rubric

For your convenience, we have included in this appendix 5-point student and teacher rubrics for each trait and scores for each Sample Paper based on the 5-point rubric. Although we have always recommended the 6-point rubric, the 5-point rubric has certain advantages.

The 5-point rubric is simple to use and to internalize. Performance is defined at only three levels: **weak** (point 1), **in process** (point 3), and **strong** or proficient (point 5). The 4 and the 2 on the 5-point scale are compromise scores. Therefore, if a performance is slightly stronger than a 3 but not quite strong enough to warrant a 5, it would receive a 4. Because raters think in terms of "weak", "in process", and "strong" in assigning scores, this is a simple system to follow.

Performance in writing is defined at only three levels, so it is possible to make those written definitions longer and more detailed than when defining *every* level. Many users like this richer text, especially if they are learning traits for the first time or if they are looking for language to use in teaching traits to students.

Few differences exist conceptually between these rubrics. Remember that the key reason to use rubrics with students is to teach the concepts: *ideas, organization, voice, word choice, sentence fluency,* and *conventions.* We want students to understand what we mean, for example, by good *organization,* and one way of doing this is to have them score writing samples. The particular rubric used is less important than whether a student sees a paper as weak, strong, or somewhere between those two points. We want students to distinguish between writing that works and writing that needs revision; whether they define a strong performance as a 5 or 6 is much less important than their understanding of why a paper is strong or weak. The numbers are merely a kind of shorthand that allows students and teachers to discuss competency in simple terms.

Keep in mind, too, that all rubrics are essentially 3-point rubrics: weak, in process, and strong. On the 5-point rubric, these performance levels correspond to the scores of 1, 3, and 5 respectively. On the 6-point rubric, each level is divided into two parts, high and low. Thus, a score of 1 represents the lower weak score, a score of 2 is a somewhat higher weak score. Scores of 3 and 4 represent the two levels of the in-process category, 5 and 6 the two levels of strength. On the 6-point rubric, *all* performance levels are defined.

We hope that these distinctions help clarify the very slight differences between these rubrics. Use the rubric with which you are most familiar or with which you feel most comfortable. Regardless of your choice, you will be teaching your students about the basic, underlying components that define good writing—and that is what counts!

Ideas

5 **My paper is clear, focused, detailed, and engaging.**

- My main idea is crystal clear throughout the paper. This writing is engaging and informative.

- The reader can tell that I know a lot about this topic.

- I chose details that are important and interesting and hold the reader's attention.

- I left out the "filler." Details relate clearly to my main idea or story.

- My topic is narrowly focused and manageable.

3 **My paper is clear enough to follow and fairly focused, but I need to include more information. Some of my details are too general.**

- I think the reader can tell what my main idea is.

- I know some things about this topic. If I knew more, I could make this really interesting and informative.

- Some of my "details" are things most people already know.

- Some information is not really needed. It's just filler.

- This topic sure feels wide—maybe I'm trying to tell too much.

1 **I'm still working on what I want to say.**

- I don't know what my main idea is. I'm still working on it.

- Help! I don't know enough about this topic to write.

- I need better details. I'm just making things up as I go.

- I'm mostly writing to fill space. I'm hoping a good topic will come to me as I write.

- I don't know whether my topic is too wide or too narrow—I'm not sure what my topic is!

Organization

5 My paper is logical and easy to follow—it's as if I'm holding a flashlight for readers.

- My lead grabs the reader's attention and makes him or her want to read on.

- Every detail seems to be in the right order.

- My paper follows a pattern that works really well for this topic.

- I built strong bridges between sentences by using transitional words.

- My conclusion brings things to closure and leaves the reader thinking.

3 The reader can follow this, I think. The light is fading—but it's there!

- My lead might need to be livelier—but at least it's there.

- Most details are in the proper order.

- I think I followed a pattern. I need to check.

- I used some transitions. They might not be strong ones though.

- My conclusion is OK. It might not make the reader think too hard, but it's there.

1 This paper is hard to follow—like walking in the dark without a flashlight!

- I don't really have a lead. I just started writing.

- I wrote things down as they came into my head. I am not sure the order works.

- I don't see any real pattern here.

- I wasn't sure how to connect ideas, so I didn't worry about transitions.

- I don't really have a conclusion. My paper just ends.

Voice

5 My voice is strong and individual. The reader can tell it's my voice!

- The reader will want to share this paper aloud.

- I love this topic, and my enthusiasm will get the reader hooked, too.

- I'm writing for a particular audience, and I've considered their interests and needs.

- I've used just the right voice for this topic. It fits like a glove.

3 You can hear me in the writing *sometimes.* My voice comes and goes.

- The reader may want to share some parts of this paper aloud.

- I couldn't get that excited about this topic; the reader can hear that in my writing.

- I thought about my audience sometimes, but not always!

- I think the voice I've used is OK for this topic.

1 I don't hear that much voice in this writing.

- The reader probably won't want to share this paper aloud.

- This topic seemed totally boring to me. I guess I sound bored, too.

- I just wanted this to be over with. I do not care if anyone reads it.

- I don't think my voice fits this topic very well. It should be stronger, or different.

Word Choice

5 **Every single word I chose helps make my message clear, memorable, and interesting.**

- Strong verbs consistently give my writing energy.

- I cut the clutter. I made every word count.

- I used sensory language to help the reader see, hear, feel, taste, or smell.

- If I used new or unusual words, I tried to make the meaning clear from context.

3 **Most words and phrases are clear. A few words may be too general—or misused.**

- Some of my verbs have power. Some could use more muscle.

- I got rid of some clutter, but this has its wordy moments.

- I missed some opportunities to use sensory language.

- I did use some new or unusual words—but I'm not sure I made their meanings clear.

1 **My words are hard to understand. I am not always sure what I'm trying to say.**

- My verbs are ordinary.

- Some parts of my writing are wordy; in other parts, I didn't say enough.

- I did not worry about sounds, smells, tastes, and feelings. I just used the first words I thought of.

- I didn't even know the meanings of all these words, so it was hard to make them clear for the reader.

Sentence Fluency

5 My writing is smooth, natural sounding, and easy to read aloud.

- The reader can easily read this aloud with the kind of expression that brings out voice and meaning.

- The reader will see plenty of variety in sentence length and structure.

- I avoided run-on sentences and repetitive or choppy writing.

- My dialogue (if I used any) sounds like real people talking.

3 Most of my writing is smooth. I might have some choppy sentences or run-ons though.

- The reader won't stumble reading this aloud. But it might be hard to get in enough expression to bring out the voice or meaning.

- A lot of my sentences begin the same way. Many are the same length, too.

- Although I revised, I may have missed some run-ons or other sentence problems.

- If I used dialogue, it needs work. Sometimes the people sound real, and sometimes they don't.

1 This is hard to read, even for me! I can't tell one sentence from another.

- I think the reader would have to work hard to read this aloud.

- It's hard to tell where my sentences begin and end. I'm not sure how long they are—or even if they begin in different ways.

- I am quite sure I have run-on sentences or other sentence problems. This needs a lot of revision before it reads smoothly.

- If I used dialogue, I do not think it is effective. It needs work.

Student Rubric for

Conventions

5 **The reader would have a hard time finding errors in this paper. It's ready to publish.**

- I used conventions correctly to make the meaning clear.

- I checked spelling, punctuation, grammar and usage, and capitalization. They are all correct.

- I read the paper silently and aloud. I corrected every mistake I saw or heard.

3 **The reader will probably notice some errors. I need to read this once more—and really be careful this time!**

- I did a lot of things just right, but I also made mistakes. Some errors might slow the reader down or make my message unclear.

- Although I checked my spelling, punctuation, grammar, and capitalization, I think there are too many errors.

- I read my paper quickly but should read it again. Maybe if I read it aloud, my ears could catch mistakes my eyes missed.

1 **I made so many mistakes that I have a hard time reading this myself.**

- This paper is so full of errors that it's hard to spot the things I did right.

- I forgot to check a lot of my spelling, punctuation, grammar, and capitalization.

- I did not read this—silently or aloud. I guess I should have.

Ideas

5 **The paper has a clear, well-focused main idea and interesting, carefully chosen details that go beyond the obvious to support or expand that main idea.**

- The main idea is easy to identify and understand. It's also well defined and small enough to be manageable.

- The writer seems to know the topic well and uses his or her knowledge to advantage.

- Details enhance the main idea and enlighten the reader.

- Unnecessary information has been omitted.

3 **The paper is clear for the most part, but the reader needs more information. Development is skeletal, or the topic may be so broad that it is hard to cover in the scope of the paper.**

- The main idea is clear or can be inferred.

- The writer seems to have a general grasp of the topic.

- Generalities abound, but a few little-known, significant, or intriguing details are also present.

- Some information is unnecessary.

1 **The writer is searching for a topic or a way to narrow a topic that is too broad to handle effectively.**

- The main idea is unclear. It is hard to figure out what the writer is trying to say.

- The writer displays limited knowledge of the topic—or it may be hard to tell what the main idea is. Or, the topic may be so broad that there is just no way to bring it into focus.

- Details seem general and random. They do not support or expand any larger message.

- Much of the writing simply fills space, as if the writer is struggling to find things to say.

Organization

5 **This paper is logical and easy to follow.**

- The lead grabs the reader's attention and sets up what follows.

- Every detail seems to come at the right time and in the right place.

- The paper follows an identifiable pattern that is well suited to the topic.

- It is easy for the reader to make connections, thanks to the writer's skillful use of transitions.

- The conclusion brings closure without being too abrupt or too drawn out.

3 **The reader can follow the direction of the paper most of the time.**

- The paper has a lead. It does not grab the reader's attention though.

- Most details come in the right order and at the right time.

- A pattern may not be immediately recognizable, but it works.

- The writer uses some transitions; some are missing or weak. Some ideas feel "tacked on" or irrelevant.

- The paper has a conclusion. It may or may not offer a strong sense of resolution.

1 **This paper is hard to follow.**

- There is no real lead. The writer just begins the paper.

- It is very difficult to connect details or thoughts to one another or to any main idea.

- It is difficult to identify any pattern within the writing.

- Transitions are weak or missing altogether.

- The paper just ends. There is no sense of closure or resolution.

Teacher Rubric for

Voice

5 The writing is highly individual. It bears the definite imprint of this writer.

- The reader will want to share this paper aloud.

- The writer seems engaged by the topic, and strong personal energy and commitment are evident in every line.

- The writer is clearly writing to a particular audience.

- The voice is totally appropriate for the topic and purpose.

3 The reader can hear the writer's voice now and again. The voice comes and goes.

- The reader might share moments aloud, even if the reader does not share the whole paper.

- The writer seems reasonably at home with the topic but less than enthusiastic. Bursts of energy mix with lulls.

- This writer *could* be writing for a particular audience—or just to get the job done.

- The voice is acceptable for the topic and audience.

1 It would be difficult to identify this writer. The voice is not powerful or strongly individual.

- This paper is not yet ready to be shared aloud.

- The writer sounds a little bored or tired; perhaps this topic did not work for him or her. It is hard to sense *any* personal engagement.

- The writer does not seem to be reaching out to any particular audience.

- The voice is not suited to the topic. It needs to be stronger— or just different in tone.

Word Choice

5 **Every word makes the writing clear and interesting.**

- Strong verbs energize the writing.

- This writing is concise. Every word counts.

- Sensory words (as appropriate) help readers see, hear, feel, taste, or smell what is happening.

- The writer makes meaning clear from context.

3 **Most words and phrases are clear; some may be vague or misused. Fine writing is weakened by fuzzy or overdone language.**

- A *few* strong verbs give life to the writing—more would help.

- Clutter makes the text wordy, or the writing is too sketchy to convey the message.

- The writer uses some sensory language—but also misses opportunities.

- Meaning is sometimes clear from context, sometimes not.

1 **Many words are hard to understand. Language has too much jargon, is too general, or is misused.**

- The writer does not rely on verbs. As a result, the language is flat or modifiers may be overdone.

- The writing may be so insufficient that it is hard to make sense of it. Or, it may be so wordy that the reader becomes overwhelmed.

- The writer does not make effective use of sensory language to help bring the topic or story to life.

- The writer does not use context to make word meanings clear. In fact, it is often difficult to determine what the writer is trying to say.

Sentence Fluency

5 The writing is smooth, natural, and easy to read aloud.

- The reader can read this with expression—like a good film script.

- Almost all the sentences begin in different ways. Some are long, some short. Variety abounds.

- The writer avoids choppy writing, ineffective repetition, or run-ons.

- If dialogue is used, it sounds like real conversation.

3 This writing features well-crafted sentences interspersed with choppy moments or run-ons.

- Although this text is fairly easy to read aloud, it may not invite the kind of expression needed to bring out the meaning or voice.

- Too many sentences begin the same way. Too many sentences are about the same length.

- Some choppy sentences, run-ons, or repetition could slow a reader down.

- Dialogue, if used, does not reflect real conversation.

1 This writing is difficult to read aloud.

- The reader will need to rehearse to read this aloud—and do some on-the-spot editing.

- It's sometimes hard to tell where sentences begin and end. Variety in sentence lengths or beginnings is minimal.

- Choppy writing, repetition, run-ons or other sentence problems abound.

- The writer may not attempt dialogue. If dialogue is used, it does not sound like real conversation.

Conventions

5 **The writer is in control of conventions, and this paper is essentially ready to publish.**

- The writer has used conventions correctly to help make the meaning clear.

- The spelling, punctuation, grammar, and capitalization are all, for the most part, correct.

- The writer has read the paper both silently and aloud and has corrected errors. It looks and sounds polished.

3 **A good, careful proofreading and editing will prepare this text for publication.**

- A few noticeable errors may slow the reader somewhat, but they do not seriously affect meaning.

- Spelling, punctuation, grammar, and capitalization are working at a functional level. Careful editing would help.

- The writer has read the paper at least once, but a second reading—silent or oral—could help reveal additional errors.

1 **This writer is not yet in control of conventions. Many errors need to be corrected before this text is ready to publish.**

- Many errors slow the reader down and get in the way of the writer's message.

- There are many errors in spelling, punctuation, grammar, and capitalization.

- The writer has not read this paper silently or aloud. It needs significant attention from the writer and (perhaps) an editing partner.

Rationales for the Scores Using the 5-point Rubric

Unit 1: Ideas

Sample Paper 1: *How to Drive Your Teacher Crazy*
Rationale for the Score

Most students should see this paper as fairly **strong.** We gave it a score of **4,** based on the 5-point rubric. It has a clear main idea: It's easy to drive your teacher crazy. The writer also includes details in the form of suggestions: make annoying noises, interrupt, and so on. It is easy to picture what the writer is talking about, although more precise details would be helpful. Still, the writer seems very engaged in the piece and encourages readers to have a good time, too.

Sample Paper 2: *Boomer*
Rationale for the Score

Most students should see this paper as **strong.** We gave it a score of **5,** based on the 5-point rubric. The writer creates a clear, vivid picture of what it is like to have a new puppy in the house. The story shows how caring for a new pet is not as simple as people sometimes think it will be. The story also shows that the writer has an exceptionally patient mother, who is willing to put up with a lot for the sake of having Boomer join the family. Notice that the writer goes beyond generalities to include specific details, such as Boomer's habits—bumping into things, chewing on everything in sight, staining the living room rug, spilling his puppy food onto the floor, and much more.

Sample Paper 3: *Dolly*
Rationale for the Score

Most students should see this paper as **in process.** We gave it a score of **3,** based on the 5-point rubric, because more information is needed to make this paper complete. The main idea could be that Hawaii is an interesting place, or it could be that swimming with dolphins is exciting. Most of the details relate to the first topic, but the title seems to suggest that the writer meant to tell something about Dolly. In addition, most of the paper is filled with generalities about Hawaii. It would be interesting to learn more about swimming with dolphins. Did Aunt Beth have fun? What skills does it take to swim with dolphins? Are dolphins friendly? The reader is left with many questions.

Sample Paper 4: *Least Favorite Chore*

Rationale for the Score

Most students should see this paper as **weak.** We gave it a score of **2,** based on the 5-point rubric, because it lacks focus and switches topics too much. The title provides a clue to the topic; the writer apparently intends to write about his least favorite chore (which seems to be washing dishes, yet cleaning his room isn't high on the list either). The paper quickly loses focus and moves on to describe the brothers' chores and how the writer wishes to have their jobs. This writer needs to pick a topic and then select details to support it.

Unit 2: Organization

Sample Paper 5: *How to Snowboard*

Rationale for the Score

Most students should see this paper as **in process.** We gave it a score of **3,** based on the 5-point rubric, because it is easy to follow and has a reasonably good lead and conclusion. The main problem is that the writer moves from one detail to another very rapidly. We never find out what a *superman* is— or what a *double black diamond* is. Ideas are only superficially connected: *The first thing, Then, One thing, Always, never, Also, Another thing.* Transitions are present, but they do not help the reader understand the "big picture." By the end, what started as an essay has dissolved into a narrative list.

Sample Paper 6: *A Day to Remember*

Rationale for the Score

Most students should see this paper as **weak.** We gave it a score of **1,** based on the 5-point rubric, because it is a collection of random thoughts with no main point. There is no real lead; the paper just begins. There is no conclusion, either; the paper simply stops. It would be very difficult to identify an organizational pattern because almost nothing connects to anything else. It could be argued that these are all "events the writer remembers." Still, the details are too general to give the piece any clear focus or sense of purpose.

Sample Paper 7: *Grizzly Bears*

Rationale for the Score

Most students should see this paper as very **strong.** We gave it a score of **5,** based on the 5-point rubric, because it is easy to follow and understand. The writer makes an important point at the beginning: There may be some surprises about grizzlies. The writer does a good job of linking details and facts to this main idea. The lead and conclusion are both strong. The writer starts by telling the reader to expect a few surprises and ends by predicting the future for grizzly bears— they won't be a problem much longer because they won't be around much longer.

Sample Paper 8: *Getting Stitches*

Rationale for the Score

Most students should see this paper as **weak.** We gave it a score of **2,** based on the 5-point rubric, because it wanders randomly and leaves to the reader the task of putting the story together. The information is there; it's just presented in a confusing order. The lead works fairly well: *Having stitches is no fun.* The writer seems to have a definite story in mind: getting stitches. But he or she is easily distracted. Furthermore, the reader is bounced from point to point—from the stitches to Todd, then to the accident, then to the experience in the hospital, and then back to the fall. There is no real ending. The paper just stops.

Unit 3: Voice

Sample Paper 9: *Lose the Hiccups*

Rationale for the Score

Most students should see this paper as **strong.** We gave it a score of **5,** based on the 5-point rubric, because it is lively and engaging. The writer creates vivid impressions of her annoyance at being unable to concentrate during the math test, the various strategies that do not work or are not practical, and the "final strategy" that takes the hiccups away. The writer seems to enjoy telling the story and invites readers to laugh along with her. The writer's voice never loses that high energy level.

Sample Paper 10: *Climbing Rocket Butte*

Rationale for the Score

Most students should see this paper as **in process.** We gave it a score of **3,** based on the 5-point rubric. The voice is not especially passionate, but it is not disinterested, either. What we miss is the insight into this writer's true feelings. Does the writer resent the fact that Ben races ahead? We suspect he does, but he doesn't really show it. How much do his feet hurt? How thirsty is he really? How rough is the terrain? Is the view at the top worth it? Many questions remain. Readers want to see, hear, and feel what's happening in this writer's world. Also, the energy seems to wind down toward the end of the paper—it reads much the way the writer apparently felt while climbing Rocket Butte.

Sample Paper 11: *Parking the Car with Dad*

Rationale for the Score

Most students should see this paper as **strong.** We gave it a score of **5,** based on the 5-point rubric. The voice is full of energy and highly individual. This paper can be seen as a character sketch, and we learn a lot about Dad: He is fussy, he's a fanatic about his car, he doesn't mind a little inconvenience if the car won't be damaged, and he assumes others (for example, Mom) will agree with his way of doing things. The specifics of what Dad does, or does not do, help the reader picture him, which is what gives the paper its strong voice.

Sample Paper 12: *Too Much Television*

Rationale for the Score

Most students should see this paper as **weak.** We gave it a score of **1,** based on the 5-point rubric. It has little or no voice; it is basically a recitation of observations. The writer sounds tired—and less than excited about this topic. The writer really seems to be filling space so that the chore of writing about television can be finished. As a result, the paper is a collection of generalities with virtually no personal insights or observations. How does this writer *really* feel about watching TV? Is he sharing the real scoop?

Unit 4: Word Choice

Sample Paper 13: *Pasta, Pasta, Pasta!*

Rationale for the Score

Most students should see this paper as **strong.** We gave it a score of **4,** based on the 5-point rubric. Though it still could use revision, it does provide some examples of good word choice. Some students may argue that the verbs could be a little stronger. This paper could also benefit from more sensory detail because it focuses on food. At the same time, the writer tells enough and tells it clearly enough that it is very easy to picture this family at dinner.

Sample Paper 14: *Autumn—My Favorite Season!*

Rationale for the Score

Most students should see this paper as **in process.** We gave it a **3,** on the 5-point rubric, even though it has some real strengths, such as the use of strong verbs: *crunching, caresses, stroll* (although *stroll* does not go with *briskly*), *fluff,* and so on. This writer also tries very hard to use sensory detail to create a rich picture of the autumn landscape. The problem is *too much* detail, and the result is overwhelming. This writer needs to pull back and focus on a *few* significant sensory details.

Sample Paper 15: *Desert Creatures*

Rationale for the Score

Most students should see this paper as very **strong.** We gave it a **5,** based on the 5-point rubric, because the word choice is striking and original: *earth's creatures, found ingenious ways, invades the desert, courtesy of nature, extracting water from what it eats,* and so on. The paper is virtually free of overused words, jargon, and clichés, and though the vocabulary is strong, it is not overdone. This is writing to inform—not to impress. Also, it is quite easy to determine the meaning of words from context. Striking word choices, including strong verbs, make this paper an excellent example of how to use words well.

Sample Paper 16: *Something I Learned to Do*

Rationale for the Score

Most students should see this paper as **weak.** We gave it a **2,** based on the 5-point rubric. By the end of the paper, it is possible to figure out what the "something I learned to do" is—framing a picture—but this is not clear at the beginning. Unclear language hides the message and makes the steps of picture framing difficult to visualize. The writer certainly overuses some words: *fun, part, things, stuff.* In addition, these words are too vague. The paper does spring to life in the last line; more of this voice and stronger word choice is needed throughout.

Unit 5: Sentence Fluency

Sample Paper 17: *Dinosaurs in the Movies*

Rationale for the Score

Most students should see this paper as **weak.** We gave it a **1,** based on the 5-point rubric, because it is filled with rambling sentences, awkward constructions ("*. . . the way they do them in the movies because first of all . . .*"), and run-on sentences ("*. . . it isn't scary anyhow if you ask me it's mostly just annoying*"). This paper sounds like stream-of-consciousness talk from a person who speaks quite rapidly and is rushing to give all the information. Notice that the only short sentences occur at the end of the paper. They're a relief after all the breathlessness!

Sample Paper 18: *Sneezing Etiquette*

Rationale for the Score

Most students should see this paper as very **strong.** We gave it a **5,** based on the 5-point rubric, because it exhibits virtually all of the qualities necessary for fluent writing. It is easy to read with expression, and oral reading helps bring out the fluency. Nearly every sentence begins differently; the variety is great. In addition, sentences vary in length, so the writing is never monotonous. The dialogue is not extensive, but what is there has a very natural sound and contributes to the fluency.

Sample Paper 19: *Seals*

Rationale for the Score

Most students should see this paper as **in process.** We gave it a **3,** based on the 5-point rubric, because there is very little variety in sentence beginnings or sentence length. Most sentences start with the words *They* or *Seals.* The writing is not difficult to follow, but it is choppy because the sentences are short and all about the same length. It would require some rehearsal to give this piece a smooth reading.

Sample Paper 20: *Birthday Gift*

Rationale for the Score

Most students should see this paper as **strong.** We gave it a **4,** based on the 5-point rubric, because the dialogue is strong. The writer and her mom have a real conversation. It sounds natural, and it also advances the story. They have a predicament—what to buy for the writer's picky friend Heather. As they decide on a gift for Heather, we learn something about the writer and her mom. Mom may be a little old-fashioned, but she's also imaginative and a good sport. She has a sense of humor, too. Sentences show a lot of variety—and the piece is easy to read aloud with expression.

Unit 6: Conventions

Sample Paper 21: *Kites*

Rationale for the Score

Most students should see this paper as **strong.** We gave it a **5,** based on the 5-point rubric, because it needs only the lightest editing. Some raters may object to the use of multiple exclamation points. This is a stylistic choice, really, and should not lower the score. This writer has done an excellent job of handling conventions effectively and making the text easy to read.

Sample Paper 22: *Traffic Flow*

Rationale for the Score

Most students should see this paper as **weak.** We gave it a **2,** based on the 5-point rubric, because it contains enough errors to slow a reader down. It will need line-by-line editing to prepare it for publication. It can be argued that, of the many errors, several involve the misspelling of the word *traffic.* If the writer corrected this one misspelling, it would significantly decrease the number of errors.

Sample Paper 23: *I Can't Believe It!*

Rationale for the Score

Most students should see this paper as **weak.** We gave it a **1,** based on the 5-point rubric, because even though the paper is quite short, it contains 36 errors. This is more than enough errors to impair readability. Moreover, there are various kinds of errors in punctuation, spelling, repeated words, unnecessary words, capitalization, and so on. This piece will require word-by-word editing to prepare it for publication.

Sample Paper 24: *I Could Swim Forever*

Rationale for the Score

Most students should see this paper as **strong.** We gave it a **5,** based on the 5-point rubric, because there is only one small error in conventions (a repeated word, *am,* in the second line). This writer uses conventions effectively to make the writing easy to read. The paper does contain sentence fragments, which add to the stylistic effect and are purposeful. Fragments aside, this paper is virtually ready for publication as is—with only one small change.